Quit Your Job & Follow Your Dreams

A 12-Month Guide to Being Joyfully Jobless

Michelle Kulp

ISBN: 978-1-7340538-1-4

TWO WEEKS IN THE SUN?
WHY NOT 52 WEEKS?

We devote not only the best years of our life, but also most of our waking hours to work. And for what? Counting the days until Friday? An employee of the month certificate? A couple of week's holiday a year? The hope that when retirement comes, we will be able to heat our homes in the winter?

There are people who are very happy in their job, who enjoy going to work every day, and who are well rewarded for their time and effort. It may even be one of their dreams to land the job they have. Good luck to them, but they aren't likely to be the one's reading this book.

Some of us seek to escape from wage slavery, and the debt, insecurity and unhappiness that comes with it, by living for the weekends. Some pretend that everything is hunky dory and have multiple credit cards and mounting debts to prove it. Others seek comfort in drink, drugs and other vices.

For decades now, we have been force fed a system that gives us bread and water when we could be dining out on milk and honey. Every day that you do a job that you hate, that neither pays you enough to fully enjoy life nor allows you to pursue the dreams that lie at the soul of your very being, you are a prisoner of that system. A Prisoner of Work.

~ Excerpt from "Get Out While You Can"
by George Marshall

"Follow your bliss and doors will open where there were no doors before." *~Joseph Campbell, author of "The Power of Myth"*

"There is a great hunger in our culture right now for meaning, for things that connect us with the world and with other people, things that really nurture the soul...."
~Bernadette Murphy, author of "Zen and the Art of Knitting"

"Most people live in survival, not in fulfillment."
~Tony Robbins, "The Power to Shape Your Destiny!"

"To find the best job in the world, sometimes you have to create it yourself." *~Jeff Taylor, founder and CEO of Monster.com*

"The best way to learn is from someone else's experience, as long as it feels real enough to be your own."
~Esther Dyson, Editor-at-Large, CNET Networks, Chairman, PC Forum

DEDICATION

This book is dedicated to my three amazing children whom I love and adore, Jason, Christine and Brittany. You all truly inspire and motivate me every day to be the best I can be! I love you all to the moon and back!

To my beautiful granddaughter, Callie Rae who brings endless joy, love, laughter and unconditional love to our family! Glamma loves you!

And to my father, William J. Bachteler, an ex-Marine, who has taught me so many life lessons. Most importantly that the example you set for others speaks volumes and is more important than the words you say. He taught me to be humble, to be grateful, to love myself, to love others and to believe in my dreams! I love you!

This book is for all the seekers out there looking for more purpose, passion and fulfillment in their lives and in their careers. Just know that what you are seeking is also seeking you!

TABLE OF CONTENTS

CUBICLE PRISON

Summer of 1999

It's 6:30 a.m.

The alarm clock jolts me awake pestering me to get out of my warm, comfy bed to prepare for my job as a Paralegal at a law firm with 600+ employees in Washington, D.C. I hit the snooze button multiple times wishing I could stay in my favorite place of all – my bed! The truth is, I wish I had a permanent snooze button so I could go back to sleep and skip work forever. Unfortunately, that's not the case.

Most mornings, I feel like a sloth. Ever so slowly I move out of my bed to begin my morning routine so I can get to the office by 9:00. I trick my body with heaps of caffeine that take me from barely alive to high functioning in a matter of minutes. I need to make breakfast, pack the lunches, feed the dog, and drop my three children at school.

Then, I've got to put on the oppressive business attire. I fantasize about staying home in my favorite pajamas and skipping the whole business suit routine; especially wearing those dreaded high heels that restrict the much-needed blood flow to my aching feet. I make the mad rush out the front door by 7:00 to get on the train for my 1½ hour commute into the city.

I'm not a morning person. Never have been, never will be. As a teenager, I loved to sleep in on the weekends until noon or so. My pops, an ex-Marine, would come into my bedroom early in the morning banging pots and pans around while screaming "Michelle, the day is half over! Rise and Shine!

You're sleeping your life away. Time to poop the poop decks. You can sleep when you're dead!"

Not sure what "poop the poop decks" had to do with anything, but what I did know was my father was interrupting my much-needed beauty rest.

Getting up before noon as a teenager was painful because I was going against my internal clock which said I needed more sleep. As an adult with loads of responsibilities, I was once again forcing myself to do something my body, mind, and soul despised doing– getting out of bed at a designated time to be at a place I didn't want to be, to do work I no longer enjoyed doing, while stuck in a cubicle for 8+ hours a day.

I was on the intolerable hamster wheel, and I didn't know how to get off.

Don't get me wrong. For many years, I loved my job at the law firm; it was a career path I had chosen during a Business Law class in my senior year of high school. I was certain I would one day become an attorney.

I went down the path to becoming an attorney but ended up taking a few detours (I married young and had three children), so I ended up with a paralegal degree and never made it to law school.

In 1983, I got my first job at a law firm performing tasks I loved doing like legal writing, legal research, interviewing clients, attending court cases, and negotiating out-of-court settlements. It was all so much fun to me! I was truly passionate about the law.

Although I hated the morning hours, I loved the work I was doing at the law firm, until one day (about a decade later) something radically changed.

The alarm clock went off at the usual time, but on this particular day, I couldn't seem to get myself out of bed no matter how hard I tried. An overwhelming sense of anxiety consumed me. Thoughts raced through my mind like "What excuse can I make to get out of work today?" "How can I stay home?" "Why do I hate my job so much?"

I called the Human Resources Department and left a voicemail while holding my nose pretending to be too sick to come to work that day. The reality was – I was sick; not physically, but mentally and spiritually. I was sick and tired of a job and career that was sucking the life out of me. I hated this job so much; all I could think of was how NOT to go to cubicle prison. I played hooky that day, stayed in my warm comfy bed and tried to figure out why I wasn't in love with my job anymore and why I couldn't force myself to get out of bed as I had done so many times before.

Too young to fully grasp that nothing lasts forever, and people fall in and out of love all the time; not just in relationships, but with careers too; I was completely baffled as to how a career I once loved was now a job I detested.

How did I go from LOVING my job to LOATHING my job and my chosen career?

The answer was TIME; time changed me, and time also changed the tasks I was performing at my job. I call this phenomena *Career Creep* which we will talk about in an upcoming chapter.

I believed whole-heartedly that this was my forever job. That nagging feeling, however, wouldn't go away. From that day forward, it required more and more of my energy just to get out of bed and go to work until one day, I couldn't force myself to do it any longer.

Unable to be my True Self in a Fake Environment

The cubicle I was assigned to at the 600+ person law firm had no natural light, no fresh air, and was the size of a walk-in closet. I spent a lot of time in "war rooms" which were designated office spaces where thousands of documents and files were stored during massive litigation cases.

I worked 8-12 hour days under artificial lights, forced air, in a cubicle with no windows, all the while pretending to be happy; until one day I couldn't breathe any longer.

I started to feel like the goldfish I had when I was a kid. Bubbles was her name, and she lived in a tiny glass bowl filled with water, fake plants, and was adorned with plastic shells and rocks. No matter how many artificial accoutrements I added to the tank, it was never going to be the real thing.

Going to the law firm every day made me feel like my little goldfish Bubbles– like a fish swimming in an artificial, too-small environment going against who I was deep inside my soul. No matter how hard I tried, I just didn't want to be there anymore. I simply couldn't fake it!

To counteract my increasing unhappiness and feelings of exhaustion, I started taking extended lunches at the nearby National Mall in DC. I found a spot under a weeping willow tree that spoke to my soul. I ditched my high heels so I could walk barefoot in the cool grass; the fresh grass breathed life into my aching feet. I fantasized about throwing my high heels into the water and ditching my law firm job forever.

Some days I imagined being five years old again and living in our little red house on Casco Street in Milford, Connecticut; climbing the apple tree in our front yard and feeling free again. My older brother Michael and I would spend our days playing outside in the yard, making tree forts, running through the sprinkler, breathing in the fresh air until it was dark outside and then catching fireflies in jars at night until our parents forced us to come inside. I loved being in nature where I always felt happy and carefree.

Suddenly, the cubicle on the 17th floor at the law firm felt like a prison that I desperately needed to escape from.

During these extended lunches to the National Mall, I basked in the warmth of the sun which seemed to breathe new life into me; even if it was just for an hour or so. I was chronically late returning to work after my stretched-out lunches. I figured sooner or later they just might fire me. The crazy part was, I really didn't care.

THE HIDDEN BLESSING

As fate would have it, I was called into a meeting one day and told, "The department you work in has been restructured and your job no longer exists."

Code for: "You're fired!"

I didn't have the courage or the cash to quit my job, so the universe helped me out.

Looking back, getting fired from my job was a blessing in disguise. At the time, however, it was terrifying to unexpectedly leave a 17-year career in the legal field with very little money in the bank (by very little, I mean none) and three young children to support as a single, divorced mom. I needed cash to pay the bills, and I needed it fast.

The three questions that consumed me were:

1. How was I going to pay the bills?

2. What could I do to make a living that was comparable to the salary I was making at the law firm?

3. Was there a way to find something I LOVED to do and that PAID the bills?

Reality set in. I had NO answers. I had NO plans. I had NO funds.

What I did have though was a massive opportunity to create a new life…and that was priceless.

A SERENDIPITOUS MEETING WITH BILLY RAY CYRUS

FROM PARALEGAL TO BESTSELLING AUTHOR, MOTIVATIONAL SPEAKER, AND 6-FIGURE ENTREPRENEUR!

Yes, that' me with Billy Ray Cyrus after a concert in 1992. Billy Ray Cyrus completely changed the trajectory of my life, so I want to share this transformational (and crazy) story with you…

My Pivotal Moment

On October 23, 1992, I met a man by the name of Billy Ray Cyrus (Country Music Singer and Actor), who changed the entire direction of my life. Some might say it was merely a coincidence, but I strongly believe it was my spiritual destiny. In 1992, I was at a very dark and desperate place in my life. My marriage had recently ended, and I was raising three children (then ages 1, 3 and 5) on my own with no financial or emotional support from my ex-husband; I was let go from the law firm where I had worked for 17 years; I was living cut-off notice to cut-off notice; and my older brother and best friend, Michael, was diagnosed with AIDS and was dying. At the time, I was also having chest pains I thought were from heart issues only to learn they were panic attacks from the chronic and severe stress I was experiencing.

Music that Spoke to my Soul

Late one evening in the summer of 1992, a neighbor stopped by and asked me if I had ever heard of Billy Ray Cyrus. Up until that point in my life, I had only listened to rock-n-roll. Growing up on 80's rock music, I was not interested or familiar with country music. My neighbor gave me a tape of Billy Ray's music and encouraged me to listen to it, especially the song, "Achy Breaky Heart." I quickly got hooked on this very addictive tune. Many nights, I blasted that song and danced around my townhouse with my three young children who also loved the song. It was a wonderful escape from my very stressed out life!

A couple of weeks later, the same neighbor reappeared to tell me that Billy Ray was playing at a concert on October 23, 1992 at the Patriot Center in Fairfax, Virginia and that I should attend. If it had been October 22nd or October 24th, I wouldn't have even thought twice about attending, but because it was October 23rd — my birthday — I felt it had a special meaning. In fact, the thought instantly popped into my head, *"Billy Ray is playing on my birthday for a reason...I am going to meet Billy Ray and he has something very important to tell me."* Perhaps all the stress was causing me to be delusional, but I honestly believed with every fiber of my being that I was going to meet Billy Ray Cyrus and that he had something important to tell me.

No Doubts, But Lots of Obstacles

Because I was 100% certain about this meeting with Billy Ray (absolutely no doubts were lingering in my mind), I purchased two tickets to the concert and recruited one of my adventurous friends to attend. The plan was simple: I would dress to stand out from the crowd (I wore a bright red spandex dress with very high red pumps), and after the concert, we would get one of the roadies to give us a backstage pass. It had worked during my teenage years to get backstage to meet the bands, so I figured it would work again.

After four failed attempts to get backstage, my friend and I were kicked out of the Patriot Center in Fairfax, Virginia and told we would be arrested if we returned. We immediately went to Plan B...which again was very simple. We would wait for Billy Ray to come out of the Patriot Center and follow his limo to the hotel where he was staying.

An hour or so later, Billy Ray finally came out; he was signing autographs and videotaping his fans...he adored his fans! We stayed in our car, ready to follow the limo. Unfortunately, we weren't the only ones with this bright idea. There were hundreds of women ready to follow the limo for a chance to meet the very handsome and very talented Billy Ray Cyrus.

This did not discourage me in the least. I drove like a maniac so I wouldn't lose sight of the limo! I cut off other drivers, ran red lights, and sped down the highway blindly following Billy Ray's limo!

I would NOT give up

We followed the limo to the Hilton Hotel where Billy Ray's bodyguard, Steve, was taking Billy Ray up to his hotel room through a side door. Luckily for me, all the other women who were following the limo jumped out of their cars and ran towards the side door of the hotel. My friend jumped out of our moving car and went inside to tell Billy Ray to wait for me because it was my birthday. I illegally parked the car in a handicapped space and ran to the elevator where Billy Ray was standing inside. Billy Ray saw me (I guess the red dress stood out!) and he took my hand and pulled me inside the elevator. I told him it was my birthday, the bodyguard snapped a picture of us, and Billy Ray autographed a tee-shirt as well as a book I had with me (*Creative Visualization* by Shakti Gawain). Maybe all the adrenaline in my body was making me have crazy thoughts, but I felt a special chemistry with Billy Ray, but before I could do or say anything, bodyguard Steve abruptly pushed me out of the elevator and told us, "Billy Ray is going up stairs now. Good night!"

In that moment, the elevator doors closed not only on me, but on my dreams! I looked at my friend and told her that whatever we did, the other women would do as well, so we need to "FAKE" leaving the hotel premises to get rid of our competition. About 10 minutes later after all the others had cleared out, my friend and I came back in; I wasn't about to give up on my dream of meeting Billy Ray Cyrus; after all, he had something important to tell me. So, we got in the elevator and pushed all the buttons. I thought that the hotel would block out the floor that Billy Ray was staying on, but they didn't – all the lights lit up!

We started at the top floor and went down

We got off the elevator on each floor and looked for clues to find Billy Ray. It didn't take us very long. On the 12th floor, I looked down the hall and saw the bodyguard, Steve, go into the last room. I was so excited! Finally, my dream was coming true. As I got near the room, bodyguard Steve heard me and came out to inform me that if I didn't leave, he was calling hotel security to have me removed. I thought I could sweet talk him into letting me see Billy Ray, but the more I talked, the more irritated and aggravated he became. I argued with him for a while until my friend told me she didn't want to get arrested and she thought we better listen to him and leave. I hesitantly left and headed back towards the elevator.

I couldn't give up at that point

I was so close. I told my friend the only thing standing between me and Billy Ray was the hallway and that I was not going to let a hallway come in between me and my dreams. Come hell or high water, I was going to figure out some way to meet Billy Ray Cyrus. So, I stood at the elevator and searched my mind for anything that would get me closer to Billy Ray. I looked up and noticed a small sign that had the room numbers printed on it, which read something like "Rooms 1200-1223" with an arrow pointing towards the direction I saw the bodyguard go. I looked across the hall and noticed a house phone on a table. I picked up the phone and dialed the last number on the sign and Voila! Billy Ray answered the phone (apparently the bodyguard was staying in a separate room). When Billy Ray answered the phone and asked who was calling, I told him it was the "Birthday Girl," to which he replied, *"You mean the girl in the red dress?"* Wow! I couldn't believe it! Billy Ray remembered who I was. He told me that he had something to tell me that I wasn't going to believe." Curiously, I waited for his explanation. He said that if there hadn't been all those women in the elevator and lobby, he would have invited me to his hotel room for some Chinese food. I told him, *"I'm here now!"*

Better Late Than Never

Billy Ray explained that he had hurt his back on stage, and that a masseuse was coming, but I could come to his room when the masseuse was done. My friend did not want to wait, so I gave Billy Ray my phone number (this was before cell phones) at the hotel where we were staying and told him to call me when he was done.

A couple of hours went by and no call from Billy Ray. Finally, I changed out of my red dress and into my pajamas, but I left my hair and make-up intact just in case he called. At about 2:00 am, I was listening to Billy Ray's music, still on an adrenaline rush, when the phone in my hotel room finally rang and it was Billy Ray! He asked me what my birthday wish was. I quickly told him, *"To meet and talk to you in person."* He said if it wasn't too late, he would love it if I would come over to his hotel and visit. I hung up the phone and I put that red dress back on and was speeding down the highway to the Hilton Hotel within minutes.

3-5 am

I arrived back at the Hilton Hotel and was heading down the hall toward Billy Ray's room when bodyguard Steve heard me and came out to investigate; he was furious. He told me to leave the hotel before he called the hotel security and the police. I swore to him that Billy Ray called and invited me to his room. I'm sure he heard that line all the time from Billy Ray's female super-fans. Luckily, Billy Ray's hotel room door was slightly ajar, and the bodyguard asked him if what I said was true. Billy Ray confirmed what I told him, so he irately let me in.

I spent the next two to three hours talking to Billy Ray (he was a complete gentleman). We spoke about our lives, our families, relationships, etc. He had a very spiritually enlightened side to him which was a stark contrast from his "stage" persona. He spoke about the fact that some people called him an "overnight success" to which he said wasn't true since he spent over ten years playing in bars to become this so-called "overnight success." I told Billy Ray my rather desperate life story. When Billy Ray looked deeply into my eyes, he said something that changed my entire life…

Dreams

Billy Ray asked me *"What are your dreams?"* To which I quickly replied, *"I don't have any dreams. My life's about survival."* Billy Ray assured me I had a dream and that I needed to go out and discover what my dream was and never, ever give up on that dream.

One year, one small book, and one BIG Dream! I took Billy Ray's advice and went out in the world for the next year searching for this elusive dream. It wasn't so easy to find my dream. I read books, talked to people, but I could not for the life of me figure out what my dream was. I kept feeling sorry for myself and thinking, "Everyone has a dream except me."

Then, one day I was at Borders Bookstore (sadly, they went out of business) when a tiny book fell into my hands that changed my life: "How to Find Your Mission in Life" by Richard Bolles. Richard Bolles also wrote a very popular book titled "What Color is Your Parachute" in which one question helped me discover my dream:

"What do you love to do where you lose all sense of time?"

Finally! I knew the answer – I loved to write! When I was younger, I would write for hours and time would fly by. When I was writing, five hours seemed like five minutes to me. That's how I knew writing was my dream. I had absolutely no concept of time when I was writing.

One Road Leads to Many Others

In 1993, I headed down that road toward my dream – to become a writer. I joined writer's groups, attended writer's conferences, and read every book about writing that I could get my hands on. Then, I wrote a manuscript titled *"Woman, take Hold of Your Power: 50 Unconscious Ways Women Give Up Their Power"* which I tried to get published for over a year. I received rejection letter after rejection letter and was becoming quite discouraged. Finally, a big New York Publishing House called and said they wanted to ask me some questions. I was so excited! I thought to myself, "Oh my God, my dreams are finally coming true!"

The man from the publishing house explained that the book I wrote was a self-help book for women and he wanted to know what my "credentials" were. He asked if I had a

Ph.D. I explained that while I didn't have a Ph.D., I had something better. He inquisitively asked, "What could be better than a Ph.D.?" To which I replied, "Life Experience. I didn't write that book from theory, but from real life stories from my personal experiences and those of my friends."

He didn't agree with me and said, "Unfortunately the publishing business is very competitive and unless you have a Ph.D., we cannot take a chance on an unknown author. It's just business. I hope you understand."

I hung up the phone feeling disappointed and excited at the same time; disappointed that they weren't going to publish my book, but excited that I finally had some confirmation from a highly credible publishing house that my writing was good enough to get published.

I never did get that manuscript published by a traditional publisher, but I did fulfill my dream when I self-published that book several years later.

How I Got Writing Credentials Without Having Any Writing Credentials.

More than anything, I wanted to be a reporter so I could obtain these "writing credentials" that the publishing house spoke about. I figured I needed them to get published and to be successful. Since I had no credentials, I had to get very creative in order to get a job as a newspaper reporter.

My plan was hatched. I decided I would simply pretend to be a reporter, attend local events, write the story, take photos and then have my father give the written story to the editor of the newspaper during his morning walk. It was a subtle way of stalking the newspaper editor and getting in the back door.

The first week after I hatched my crazy plan, the editor published my story on the front page. At this point, I had never spoken with him. I was shocked and ecstatic. I did this for four more weeks in a row and every week he prominently published my articles in the newspaper. Finally, I got a call from the editor of the newspaper and in an irritating tone he asked, "What? Do you want a job or something?"

He was a large, intimidating and controversial guy from Scotland that some people loved, but a lot more people hated. I told him on the phone that I might want a job, so he invited me to come in and talk to him.

When I arrived at the newspaper headquarters, he asked me to shut the office door so no one could hear our conversation. He said annoyingly, *"You see all those reporters out there? Well, I have to do a lot of editing when they turn in their stories!"* I timidly replied *"Isn't' that what editors do?"*

"Yes, but my point is your writing is good and I don't have to edit it."

Wow! What a compliment! I was floored to say the least. Not long after, the editor of the newspaper offered me a full-time position with benefits as a reporter.

Unfortunately, when I learned the salary was half what I was making as a paralegal, I had to decline. Thankfully, we made a deal that I would be a freelance reporter for the newspaper, and he would pay me per article. It was perfect because as a freelancer, I could now get the "writing credentials" I needed as well as create a new stream of income to support myself and my three children.

The dream of becoming a writer led me to other roads I would have never imagined myself on – I became a motivational speaker, a workshop leader, an online entrepreneur, and a book launch expert.

It's actually hard to believe I am a speaker as I spent seven long years overcoming my intense fears of public speaking (that's a whole other book). But deep down, I knew that if I was ever going to become a successful writer, I had to get over my fear of public speaking. I believed I was being judged harshly by others and didn't feel worthy enough to share my voice with the world. I finally overcame that fear and now I happily share my stories on stage in front of hundreds and sometimes thousands of people.

LISTENING TO MY INNER VOICE HELPED ME NOT JUST SURVIVE BUT THRIVE

Instead of listening to my fears that were trying to keep me safe and small, I began listening to soul and my inner voice. I began to appreciate my resourcefulness, creativity, determination, my ability to think outside the box, and my risk-taking skills, which some people refer to as "insanity" or "leaping without a net."

Living my Dream

I am living the life I dreamed of many years ago. I have a fulfilling business that I love. I work 20-25 hours a week and have a rewarding 6-figure income. Most importantly, I have FREEDOM. I am living my dreams of writing, coaching, and speaking which fills my soul. I talk to so many people on a weekly basis who are unhappy with their jobs and who are killing themselves to pay the bills, and I want to help them find and live their dreams.

John O'Donohue, Irish poet and Catholic Scholar, reminds us:

"To be born is to be chosen. No one is here by accident. Each one of us was sent here for a special destiny."

So, what is *your* special destiny?

CONFESSIONS OF A SERIAL QUITTER

I have a confession to make. **I AM A QUITTER.**

That's right. I am an expert at quitting jobs.

Before I was 25 years old, I estimate that I had about 20 or 30 jobs. Sounds crazy, but it's true!

I repeated this pattern for many years, so it seems only natural to be writing a book teaching others how to *QUIT THEIR JOBS & FOLLOW THEIR DREAMS*.

By "quitting" things I didn't like,
it actually brought me closer
to what I did like.

I didn't set out in life to be a Quitter; it's just that I had a low tolerance for:

- Boring work
- Low pay
- Office politics
- Bosses (or anyone) telling me what to do
- Long hours
- Stress
- Long commutes
- Cubicles with no sunlight or fresh air
- Corporate BS

Maybe you can relate?

Every day, the majority of people I meet tell me how much they "hate" their jobs.

In my younger years, when I was a serial job hopper. I would see a job advertised that I thought sounded great, apply, get hired, and then realize a day, a week or even a month later, that I actually hated it!

Looking back, I'm glad I had such a low tolerance for "*job misery*" because I believe that trait is what has made me successful today. It forced me to try new things, take risks, get comfortable with uncertainty, fail, and helped me gain the clarity about who I was and what I liked and didn't like. Over time, this is what helped me discover my dreams and passions.

In his bestselling book, "Range: Why Generalists Triumph in a Specialized World," author David Epstein talks about generalists as people who find their path late in life, and who juggle many interests rather than focusing on one. He calls this exploratory time "sampling," and the people who do this are "samplers."

I didn't realize until I read his book and met him at the National Book Festival that I was a sampler. I was happy to learn that David's research shows people who try a lot of different things actually end up with more fulfilling and successful careers.

I'm glad I was a quitter of jobs (and careers and hobbies) and not afraid to be a sampler. As we go through this journey, I want you to keep in mind that it's okay to be a sampler and a quitter because that actually moves you closer to finding your passion and creating work you love.

In his book, David Epstein shares his doubts about changing careers and jobs:

"I was working on a scientific research vessel in the Pacific Ocean after college when I decided for sure that I wanted to be a writer, not a scientist. I never expected that my path from science into writing would go through work as the overnight crime reporter at a New York City tabloid, nor that I would shortly thereafter be a senior writer at Sports Illustrated, a job that, to my own surprise, I would leave. I began worrying that I was a job-commitment-phobic drifter who must be doing this whole career thing wrong. Learning about the advantages of breadth and delayed specialization has changed the way I see myself and the world."

David goes on to say that the challenge we all face is how to maintain the benefits of breadth, diverse experience, interdisciplinary thinking and delayed concentration in a world that increasingly incentivizes, even demands, hyper-specialization.

I'm giving you permission to be a sampler, to try new things, and to quit things that you don't enjoy.

Although early specialization has faster short-term benefits, David Epstein shows through his research that "slow bakers" or "late developers" are more successful long term and will increasingly thrive.

MULTIPLE INTERESTS AND MULTIPLE STREAMS OF INCOME

Having multiple streams of income is a great way to pursue different passions and interests and also to make more money than with just one stream. Moreover, it's good to have multiple streams in case one stream dries up, you have others coming in!

After I left the legal field, I started creating multiple streams of income.

Because I love teaching, I decided to start my online business, Become a 6-Figure Woman, in 2005—www.becomea6figurewoman.com. I ran my online business part time while creating multiple streams of income. I created and sold digital online courses and also did private coaching. Over the years, I did a variety of things to generate income like website design, copywriting, and SEO (search engine optimization). These skills became very important later when I started my next business.

In 2013, I launched another business and website, www.bestsellingauthorprogram.com to help authors and entrepreneurs write, publish, promote, and profit from a bestselling book. I used all of the skills I had acquired from my legal, sales, and journalism careers to launch this new program. Using skills we've learned throughout our lives and then putting them together to create something new can be very lucrative. I call this "skill-stacking" and it can make you a lot of money.

When I'm not working on my client's books, I write my own books as well. I've published eight books as of the time of this writing.

I haven't had a 9 to 5 corporate job since 2000. I often work in my jammies or yoga clothes, my commute is from my bedroom to my office overlooking the beautiful Chesapeake Bay, and I feel blessed to get paid to do what I LOVE!

When you spend years in a job you hate, it feels so good to be your own boss and do what you love – and to also make money doing that.

I wake up without an alarm clock and start my day in a very relaxed way: meditation, journaling, yoga, a cup of English breakfast or Earl Grey tea, a leisurely walk in the neighborhood, and just ease into the day. I sometimes have lunch or dinner with my kids, family and friends, and go on mini-adventures and beach trips. I love spending time with my beautiful grand-daughter, Callie Rae!

I am so grateful to have a 6-figure income and to be living my dreams. I want to teach you how to do the same because I know how it feels to be STUCK in a job you hate and think like there's no way out. I can't wait to show you how to create a life and work you LOVE so that you can be paid for your passions, gifts and talents.

Even though I was miserable at the end of my 17-year legal career, I didn't leave voluntarily because of these three reasons:

1. Massive fears

2. Uncertainty about the future

3. Money worries

Fear, uncertainty, and money worries kept me stuck in a job I hated and "getting fired" was the universe telling me I was in the wrong job and that it was time for a change.

It's important to understand that just because you want to quit your job doesn't mean that you made a mistake taking that job, that you are a failure, or that you've wasted time in the wrong job.

Soren Kierkegaard, a German Philosopher once said:

"Life can only be understood backwards; but it must be lived forwards."

I promise that you will use **ALL** of the skills you have learned so far in your life as you venture off in new directions to *follow your dreams*.

As I said earlier, I use many of the skills I obtained from my past jobs in my online business. In fact, I am thankful for all of my corporate-world skills like legal writing, legal research, as well as technology, communication, organizational, and sales skills. I am especially grateful I can type 100 words per minute as it comes in handy in the publishing field.

The key to creating a happy life is being able to recognize when you are off course from your authentic path (the one where you feel fulfilled, on purpose and passionate about) and to make small shifts that bring you back to your true, authentic path.

This book is designed to help get you back to that authentic path and rediscover what makes you happy, what brings you joy, and to recognize that you can be well paid for doing things you love. In fact, it's easier now more than ever to create work you love and that brings you deep fulfillment.

Most people spend their entire lives building somebody else's dreams…this book is about learning to put yourself first and to *START BUILDING YOUR DREAMS*.

Quitting your job is a huge risk, but it's time to get out of your comfort zone because:

COMFORT IS DEATH

So, together let's take the journey back to the real YOU…

The Pros and Cons to Quitting Your Job & Following
Your Dreams:

Pros	Cons
Living More Authentically	Leaving a Secure position can be terrifying
Living a more meaningful life	The road will, without a doubt, be difficult
The opportunity to do what you LOVE!	You must face failure and rejection
Feeling Spiritually Fulfilled	Receiving Disapproval from others
Inspiring others to follow their dreams	Self-doubt
More Control of your Time and Income	Sacrificing the luxuries (for a while)
Living BIG	Living Little
Being Happy	Being Miserable

PART I - CLARITY

"Clarity about what matters provides clarity about what does not."

~Cal Newport, author of *Deep Work*

CHAPTER 1

THE FOUR DISTINCTIONS - JOB, CAREER, HOBBY, CALLING

"While your career is about a relationship between you and the world; your vocation is about the relationship between you and God. Vocation is a private vow. Your career is dependent upon other people, but your vocation belongs only to you. You can get fired from your career, but you can never get fired from your vocation."

~Elizabeth Gilbert, from the book *Big Magic*

Most people are searching for more purpose and more meaning in their lives. I'm sure it's why you are reading this book. There is a lot of confusion about purpose, passion and meaning, and I think it's because so many of us confuse these four words: **Job, Career, Hobby, and Calling.**

When I was in college studying law, I worked as a cocktail waitress at the Sheraton Hotel – that was my **JOB,** and it paid the bills. After I graduated from college, I worked for 17 years as a paralegal and legal secretary – that was my **CAREER**. I love baking and cooking – that is my **HOBBY**. My passion is writing, and that is my **CALLING**.

Do you see the distinctions I made?

Elizabeth Gilbert, author of the NY Times bestselling book, *Eat Pray Love* and *Big Magic,* wrote a blog post about these four important distinctions between a job, a career, a hobby and a calling and I wanted to share her post with you as we begin our journey together…

Elizabeth Gilbert's blog post:

"Dear Ones - I get a lot of questions from people who are seeking purpose and meaning in their lives. And I get a lot of questions from people who are seeking career advice – especially about creative careers. And I get a lot of questions from people who are absolutely confused about where their energy is going in life, and why.

For anyone out there who is seeking purpose and meaning and direction in their lives, I thought it might be useful today to define and differentiate four very important words that relate to **HOW WE SPEND OUR TIME IN LIFE.**
Are you ready?

The four very important words are:

1. HOBBY

2. JOB

3. CAREER

4. VOCATION/CALLING

These four words are often interconnected, but they are NOT interchangeable.

Too much of the time, we treat these words like they are synonyms, but they are NOT. They are gloriously distinct and should remain gloriously distinct. Each is wonderful and important in its own way. I think a lot of the pain and confusion that people face when they are trying to chart their lives is that they don't understand the meaning of these words — or the expectations and demands of each word.

So, let me break down what I consider to be the definitions and differences.

1) **HOBBY** — A hobby is something that you do for pleasure, relaxation, distraction, or mild curiosity. A hobby is something that you do in your spare time. *Hobbies can come and go in life* — you might try out a hobby for a while, and then move on to something new. I grew up in a family where everyone had hobbies (my grandmother made rag rugs; my grandfather made jewelry out of old spoons; etc.) and I have hobbies myself. Gardening was my hobby a few years ago; now it's Karaoke and collage-making. You can tell when something is a hobby because your attitude toward it tends to be *relaxed* and *playful*. The stakes are SUPER low with hobbies. Sometimes you might make a bit of money out of your hobby, but that's not the point — nor does it need to be. Hobbies are important because they remind us that not everything in life has to be about productivity and efficiency and profit and destiny. Hobbies are mellow. This is a wonderful reminder, and the concept should relax you. Hobbies prove that we have spare time — that we are not just slaves to the capitalist machine or to our own ambitions. You don't NEED a

hobby, mind you, but it's awfully nice to have one. Even the word itself is adorable and non-threatening: HOBBY! What a cute word. Go get one. You have nothing to lose, and it'll probably make you happier. Also, my grandparents would approve. Back before TV, everyone had hobbies. It's nice. No big deal.

2) **JOB** – You may not *need* a hobby, but you do absolutely *need* a job. Unless you have a trust fund, or just won the lottery, or somebody is completely supporting you financially... you need a job. Actually, I would argue that even if you DO have a trust fund or a winning lottery ticket or a generous patron, you should still have a job. I believe there is great dignity and honor to be found in having a job. A job is how you look after yourself in the world. I always had a job, or several jobs, back when I was an unpublished, aspiring writer. Even after I'd already published three books, I still kept a regular job, *because I never wanted to burden my creativity with the responsibility of paying for my life.* Artists often resent having jobs, but I never resented it. Having a job always made me feel powerful and secure and free. It was good to know that I could support myself in the world, and that I would never starve, no matter what happened with my creativity. **Now, here's the most essential thing to understand about a job: IT DOESN'T HAVE TO BE AWESOME.** Your job can be boring, it can be a drag, it can even be "beneath you". Jobs don't need to be soul-fulfilling. Really, they don't. I've had all kinds of weird and lame jobs; it doesn't matter, you don't need to love your job; you just need to have a job and do it with respect. Of course, if you absolutely hate your job, by all means look for another one, but try to

be philosophical about why you have this job right now. (Some good philosophical reasons for staying in a crappy job right now include: You are taking care of yourself; you are supporting your beloved family; you are saving up for something important; you are paying off debts. The list of reasons to have a job — even a bad job — goes on and on, and honor abides within all those reasons.) Don't judge yourself about your job and never be a snob about anyone else's job. We live in a material world and everyone has to do something for money, so just do whatever you have to do, collect your paycheck, and then go live the rest of your life however you want. Your job does not need to be how you define yourself; you can create your own definitions of your purpose and your meaning, pulled from deep within your imagination. A job is vital, but don't make it YOUR LIFE. It's not that big a deal. It's just a job — a very important and also not-at-all important thing.

3) **CAREER** — A career is different from a job. A job is just a *task* that you do for money, but a career is something that you **build over the years with energy, passion, and commitment**. You don't need to love your job, but I hope to heaven that you love your career — or else you're in the wrong career, and it would be better for you to quit that career and just go find yourself a job, or a different career. Careers are best done with excitement. Careers are huge investments. Careers require ambition, strategy, and hustle. Your career is a relationship with the world. I used to have jobs, but now I have a career. My career is: AUTHOR. That means: Professional Writer. When I think about my work in terms of my career, I need to make sure that I'm building good

relationships in the publishing world, and making smart decisions, and managing myself well within a realm that is more public than private. I need to pay attention to what critics are saying about my work, and how my books are selling, and how well I'm meeting my deadlines. I need to tend to my career with respect and regard, or else I will lose it. I need to honor my contracts and my contacts. When I make decisions about my life, I need to think about whether this would be good or bad for my career. If I win an award, that's good for my career. If I get caught in a hotel room with a pile of cocaine and six exotic dancers, that's bad for my career. (Actually, now that I think about it, maybe that would be AWESOME for my career! Gotta look into that! HA!) Let me make something very clear about careers: **A career is a good thing to have if you really want one, but YOU DO NOT NEED TO HAVE A CAREER.** There is absolutely nothing wrong with going through your entire life having jobs, and enjoying your hobbies, and pursuing your vocation, but never having "a career". A career is not for everyone. A career is a choice. But if you do make that choice, make sure that you really care about your career. Otherwise, it's just an exhausting marathon, for no reason. I really care about my career, but it's not the most important thing in my life. Not even close. The most important thing in my life is my....

4) **VOCATION** − The word "vocation" comes to us from the Latin verb "vocare" − meaning "*to call*". *YOUR VOCATION IS YOUR CALLING.* Your vocation is a summons that comes directly from the universe and is communicated through the *YEARNINGS OF YOUR SOUL.*

While your career is about a relationship between you and the world; your vocation is about the relationship between you and God. Vocation is a private vow. Your career is dependent upon other people, but your vocation belongs only to you. You can get fired from your career, but you can never get fired from your vocation. Writing was my vocation long before I was lucky enough to get the career of an "Author" – and writing will always be my vocation, whether my career as an Author keeps working out or not. This is why I can approach my career with a certain sense of calm – because I know that, while I obviously care about career, I am not defined by it. When I consider my writing in terms of my career, I have to care what the world thinks about me. But when I consider my writing in terms of my vocation, **I TRULY DO NOT GIVE A FUCK WHAT THE WORLD THINKS ABOUT ME.** My career is dependent upon others; my vocation is entirely my own. The entire publishing world could vanish, and books could become obsolete, and I would still be a writer – because that's my vocation. That's my deal with God. *You do not need to make money from your vocation in order for it to have meaning.* Writing had meaning for me LONG before you ever heard of me, and long before anyone else wanted me to do it.

Vocation has nothing to do with money, with career, with status, with ambition. I often see people corrode their vocation by insisting that it become a career – and then making career decisions that destroy their vocation. (Amy Winehouse's career destroyed her vocation, for instance.) The day that I feel my career is destroying my vocation, I will quit my career and go get a job, so that I can protect my vocation. But

I will never quit my vocation. Nobody even needs to know about your vocation, in order for it to have meaning. Your vocation is holy because it has nothing to do with anyone else. *Your vocation can be anything that brings you to life and makes you feel like your soul is animated by purpose.* Tending to your marriage can be your vocation. Raising your children can be your vocation. Teaching people how to take care of their health can be your vocation. Visiting your elderly neighbors can be your vocation. I have a friend who finds his vocation in picking up garbage off the streets wherever he goes; this is his gesture of love toward his fellow man. Searching for light and peace and meaning can be your vocation. Forgiveness can be your vocation. Brother Lawrence was a 17th century monk who worked his whole life washing dishes in a monastery (because washing dishes was his JOB) but his vocation was to see God in everything and everyone, and that is why he radiated grace. (Awesome vocation, by the way. People came from all over the world to watch Brother Lawrence wash dishes, because of the way he radiated divine love in every act. THAT'S vocation.) I admire the Roman Catholic Church for understanding the sanctity of vocation, and for teaching that the purest human vocation is LOVE. A vocation is the highest expression of your human purpose, and therefore you must approach it with deepest reverence. You can be called to your vocation by what you love (for instance: I love writing), or you can be called to your vocation by what you hate (for instance: I know people who dedicate themselves to social justice because of their hatred for violence and inequality.) If you don't have a vocation and you long for one, you can pray for one. You can ask the universe with humility to lead you to your vocation – but then you must pay VERY close attention to the clues and signs that point you toward your vocation. **Don't just pray and WAIT. Instead, pray and**

SEEK. Everyone wants the lightning strike, but the path to your vocation is usually a trail of bread crumbs, instead. Look for clues. No clue is too small; no vocation is insignificant. Don't be proud; be attentive. **What brings your soul to life?** What makes you feel like you are not just a meat puppet – not just here to work hard and pay bills and wait to die? You cannot be lazy or entitled about your vocation, or apathetic, or fatalistic, or calculating. You cannot give up on it, if things don't "work out" – whatever that even means. You must work closely with your intuition in order to find your highest meaning in life. This is hard work sometimes, but it is divine work, and it is always worth it. (Here's a possibility, for instance: Searching for your vocation can be your vocation!) You can choose your hobbies, your jobs, or your careers, but you cannot choose your vocation; you can only accept the invitation that has been offered to you or decline it. You can honor your vocation, or you can neglect it. You can worship it, or you can ignore it. A vocation is offered to you as a sacred gift, and it is yours to care for, or to lose. When you treat your vocation as sacred, you will see your whole life as sacred – and everyone else's lives, too. When you are careless about your vocation, you will treat your whole life carelessly -– and other people's lives, too. Your vocation will become clear to you through the act of **PAYING ATTENTION** to your senses and your soul, and to what in the world causes you to feel love or hate. You will be led to your vocation, though the path is not always obvious. You must participate in its unfolding. Do not fall asleep on this job. Your vocation is **hinted** at through your talents, tastes, passions, and curiosities. Your vocation is calling you, even when you can't quite hear it. (*"What you are seeking is seeking you" – Rumi*.) When you embrace a vocation, and commit yourself to that vocation, your mind becomes a quieter place. When you accept the divine invitation of your vocation, you will become strong. You will know that – as long as you are tending to your vocation – everything will be fine.

My feeling is that people look for purpose in life without understanding these four words: HOBBY, JOB, CAREER, VOCATION. People blend these four concepts, or mistake them, confuse them, or try to have all four at once, or pretend that they are all the same thing. Or people just generally get freaked out and confused, because they haven't thought these words through, or decided which ones are most important. (Or which ones are most important RIGHT NOW.) People generally want to know, "*What am I doing with my life?*", but they don't slow down long enough to really think about these four different aspects of this question – the four different possibilities for where our time and energy goes. People worry so much about their careers, for instance, that they often forget to pay attention to their vocations. Or people get so seduced by the grandeur of their vocations that they forget to have a job, and so they stop taking care of themselves and their families in the material world...which will only bring suffering. (Remember: Even Brother Lawrence had a job. He was not too proud to wash dishes.) Or people are so busy chasing social status and personal advancement that they forget to make time for the relaxing joy of having a sweet little hobby. And oftentimes people mistake a sweet little hobby for something that they think should be a job, or a career, or a vocation. **Don't try to blend what perhaps doesn't need to be blended. Don't mistake a job for a career, or a career for a vocation, or a vocation for a hobby, or a hobby for a job. Be clear about what each one is and be clear about what can be reasonably expected from each one and be clear about what is demanded of you with each one.**

Here's another thing I see happening: people get so embarrassed or resentful about their lousy day jobs that they forget to be grateful that they have a job at all – and this causes only more anxiety and confusion, which again, will make them stop paying reverent attention to their vocation, or enjoying their hobbies, or making plans for a career.

We live in a real world that is heavy sometimes with real-life obligations, but we also have souls that deserve care and attention. We can pay attention to our worldly ambitions and pleasures (hobbies, jobs, careers) without neglecting our mystical, otherworldly, beautiful and often impractical vocations. We can pay attention to all of it – but this requires sitting still at times and really thinking things through, with courage and dignity. And it requires an understanding of terms.

The important thing is to be sober and careful and attentive enough to know what you are REALLY talking about when you consider the question, *"What am I doing with my life?"*

It isn't easy to answer this question but understanding and respecting these four different words might be a start.

And when in doubt, at least *try* SOMETHING. As the wonderful poet David Whyte says: *"A wrong-headed but determined direction is better than none at all."*

Good luck out there, brave seekers!

Onward,

LG

****

My Own Confusion About The Four Distinctions

I love Elizabeth Gilbert's post because it helped bring clarity to my own life. I can see now how I tried to *blend things* that didn't need to be blended. At different times in my life, I tried to blend hobbies into jobs (jobbies) which didn't work out because it took all the fun out of it. I've also been resentful of some of the jobs I had because they weren't "lighting me up," however, I see now that I lacked gratitude for the fact that my job was actually supporting me and my family.

As I said earlier, my CALLING is writing. I do it in a variety of ways such as writing books, blog posts, online courses, articles, and talks. It took me a long time to figure this out, but I know in my heart and soul that I have been called to write. It's my *natural gift and it is what I LOVE doing!*

In this chapter, we are going to look back in your life to see how these four distinctions have played out.

First, I want to take what Elizabeth Gilbert said about "JOBS" in her post and make one more distinction between what I call a **FREEDOM JOB** and a **BONDAGE JOB**.

This is a distinction I feel is important to make because I've had both types of jobs and having a **FREEDOM JOB** is much better than being stuck in a **BONDAGE JOB**.

A **FREEDOM JOB** is a "drop-out" job that doesn't sap your spirits and suck up all your time and energy. You need time and energy to pursue your hobbies and to discover your calling. A freedom job covers most or all of your expenses and some extra but does not consume or define you.

A **FREEDOM JOB** is important because you need time, space and energy to explore your passions and curiosities. When you have a **FREEDOM JOB,** then you do what you have to do to pay the bills *without* giving away your soul. You want to save your energy for what you really want to do (or figuring out what you really want to do if you don't know what that is yet).

Remember, your vocation for a while might be figuring out what your vocation is; and that's okay. The point is: you need energy and space to figure out your passions, and a **FREE-DOM JOB** will give you that.

My **FREEDOM JOB** after I was fired from the law firm was an outside sales job that I had for 10 years. I worked 20-25 hours per week, made six figures selling hot tubs, and had lots of time and energy to pursue my interests and passions. It wasn't draining to my soul like my legal job was at the end.

You can also think of your **FREEDOM JOB** like a bridge taking you from one side of the river to the other. The river you're heading to is a life of creativity, passion, fulfillment, and joy. It might not be your forever job, but it will take you where you want to go – MOVING you towards your dreams and your vocation.

A **BONDAGE JOB,** on the other hand, consumes your time, energy, and life force. A big part of why you might be feeling *stuck* when it comes to figuring out what your dreams are is because you don't have the time or energy required to do it.

Part of this journey is creating time in your life to day-dream, try new things out, and discover renewed things about yourself. Unfortunately, if you're in a **BONDAGE JOB**, then your job has your time and energy.

Think about this:

IT'S HARD TO ASSESS YOUR LIFE
WHEN YOUR JOB IS YOUR LIFE.

I'm not sure where you are in your life right now, but if you are working in a **BONDAGE JOB**, then the first goal for you is to transition from this **BONDAGE JOB** to a **FREEDOM JOB** so you can create space, time, and energy in your life to discover what you want at the deepest level of your being.

Elizabeth Gilbert said in her blog post:

*"Everyone wants the lightning strike,
but the path to your vocation is usually a
trail of bread crumbs, instead.
Look for clues. No clue is too small."*

To create your dream life, we need to find clues to your dreams.

I've created what I call **"Treasure Map Exercises"** throughout this book to give you deeper insight in putting together clues that will give you the answers you are seeking.

I recommend getting a special notebook or journal so you can do these exercises and record them all in one place where you can look back at them.

Let's get started with our first TREASURE MAP EXERCISE. When you see this image below throughout the book, that means there is an exercise coming up. Doing these exercises will help move you closer to creating your dream life. At the end, you'll put all the clues together and find your own treasure!

THE FOUR DISTINCTIONS IN YOUR OWN LIFE

It's your turn now to look at the four distinctions in your own life.

Answer the questions below in your notebook or journal. The goal is to take an inventory of your hobbies, careers, jobs, and vocations so that you can get a birds-eye view of them. Maybe you've never had a career, but only a series of jobs. That's okay. Maybe you don't know what your vocation (calling) is and that's okay too. Just write down what you have experienced in your life so far.

My hobbies are (or have been):

_____

_____

_____

_____

_____

My *BONDAGE jobs are (or have been):

_____

_____

_____

_____

_____

My *FREEDOM jobs are (or have been):

_____

_____

_____

_____

_____

My Careers are (or have been):

_____

_____

_____

_____

_____

My Vocations (Callings) are (or have been):

_____

_____

_____

_____

_____

Take some time to reflect on what you've written.

Do you think you've tried to blend things that didn't need blending like Elizabeth Gilbert spoke about in her blog post? Did you have a lot of bondage jobs?

I recommend doing this exercise for as many jobs, careers, callings, and hobbies as you can think of. This will give you a new perspective as you travel down memory lane and take a deeper look at your past.

Your past is what led you to this point in time right now. So, if you're feeling unfulfilled, unhappy, miserable, and miles off your authentic path, this will give you clues and the much-needed insight as to how you got there.

My father who is a big history buff says, *"If you don't know your history, you're bound to repeat it."* It's important to know your history to avoid repeating patterns.

I recommend the *Observation without Condemnation* approach when you're looking at your life and implementing changes. Don't condemn yourself for your past choices. You did the best you could with the knowledge, skills, and aware-ness you had.

As the wonderful Maya Angelou once said, "Do the best you can until you know better. Then when you know better, do better."

We are looking at where you've been so we can see what worked and acknowledge what didn't work so well. From that place, with a new perspective, we can make changes.

Once you've examined your own four distinctions regard-ing jobs, careers, hobbies and callings, in the next chapter, you are going to complete a **Job Autopsy** to deepen your under-standing about your past jobs.

CHAPTER 2

PERFORMING A JOB AUTOPSY

A job has many parts to it like the tasks that we do, the hours we work, the people we interact with, the salary, the benefits, as well as intangible things like feeling appreciated, respected and valued.

At the end of my 17-year legal career, I was deeply confused about why a job I once loved became a job I absolutely despised.

It's easy to say, "I hate my job," but understanding *why* you hate your job will give you the insight you need to make changes.

My daughter was working in an outside sales job and was considering a job change. When I asked her why she hated her job, she complained about the hours being too early. I asked her if she was able to change the hours, would she want to stay at her job. Surprisingly, her answer was "YES." As she thought about it more, she realized there were several aspects of her job that she loved such as:

- Not being stuck in an office all day
- Driving a company vehicle
- Meeting new people
- Earning high commissions
- Generating her own leads
- Paid time off and vacations
- Great health insurance
- Stability

She ended up getting fired from this job because she was consistently late to meetings. As she contemplated her next move, she decided she wanted to start her own painting company because what was truly missing in her last job was creativity and freedom. Before the sales job, she had worked as painter for five years for a government contractor, so she had the skills needed to start her own company. And now she is very happy painting as a subcontractor and has more freedom and creativity than she has ever had.

Doing a **JOB AUTOPSY** will give you a deep understanding about what you love and what you don't enjoy when it comes to work. Think of yourself as a private detective looking for clues from your past that you will use to greatly improve your future.

A JOB AUTOPSY can help you determine if implementing some changes at your current job would be enough to make your job more satisfying (at least for the time being) while you do this exploratory work.

You can make your current job more bearable and satisfying now while you look for another job.

MAYBE YOU JUST NEED SOME CAREER PATH RESUSCITATION (CPR)

Doing this deep work using the job autopsy exercises will help you figure out how you can breathe new life into your current job. For some people, making some changes at their current job will make things more bearable during this transition.

So today is the day that you are going to start taking back your power by gaining more satisfaction from your current job which is going to require two things on your part:

- Purposeful action

- Setting your intention

Beverly Kaye and Sharon Jordan-Evans, authors of *Love it, Don't Leave It: 26 Ways to Get What You Want at Work*, say:

"Too often we leave for greener pastures elsewhere only to find Astroturf."

You know my story now of how I had been a serial job-hopper for many years. I wanted to try new things and quite frankly, I think I liked the *chase* more than I liked the actual jobs I was chasing. However, the reality is I didn't know whether I liked a job until I actually tried it out.

Experience is what helped me figure things out.

Trying new jobs and experiences is a great way to gain more clarity. We get into trouble when we aren't happy at a job and we choose to stay there for years suffering needlessly.

Being a paralegal was my passion and career for many years and I loved it! I was a serial job hopper in the legal field because it was the best way I knew how to get a raise. And because I was a single mom living paycheck-to-paycheck, money for me was the driving factor.

In the late 1990s, I started feeling burnt out in the legal field; I had lost the passion I once had for my job and my job felt meaningless and stressful. I knew I wanted out but didn't know how to get out.

I didn't have any of the tools like the ones I'm sharing with you here.

Many people change jobs in their chosen field only to find out it doesn't fix the deeper problem– that you've lost your passion and meaning in that field.

One of the things I learned about myself after leaving the legal field is that I am a people person and I didn't enjoy long hours at the computer away from human connection. At the time, I was spending 80-90% of my day at the computer – no wonder I was so miserable!

What's interesting is that when I first began my career as a paralegal, I worked for a solo practitioner where I spent 60% of my day interviewing clients, doing new case intakes, interacting with clients, insurance adjustors, attorneys, court personnel, etc. I stayed at that job for over five years (which was a record for me). I loved so much about that job.

So why did I leave the job that I loved at the small law firm?

MONEY

I went to the large law firms in Washington, D.C. because they paid more and offered better benefits, and that's when it happened:

CAREER CREEP

Marcus Buckingham, co-author of, *One Thing You Need to Know* defines Career Creep as:

"Following your initial success, one new responsibility is added, then another, then another, as your job slowly shifts beneath you, inching you further and further away from your strengths' path until finally, you wake up one morning and realize that the majority of your new job bores you, leaves you unfulfilled, frustrates you, drains you, or all of the above."

Sound familiar?

Over a period of several years, I started doing less and less of what I loved (interacting and engaging with people; legal writing and research, etc.) and more and more of what I didn't love (working on a computer, filing papers, making copies). Essentially, I traded in what I LOVED for more MONEY.

This is how I lost meaning: by following the money and making all my decisions based on this one factor.

When I got fired from the law firm at the end of my 17-year career, I can honestly say I was spending 95% of my day doing tasks I didn't like.

Because I was a struggling single parent of three trying to make ends meet, I couldn't just ditch my job because I wasn't happy. I had responsibilities and obligations. I felt trapped. I wanted more than anything to wave a magic wand and NOT to have to go to that dreaded job and still be able to take care of my family. I didn't quit because I didn't know what else to do to make money, so I settled for job misery.

I settled because I felt stuck; it felt like
I had NO other options at the time.

Do you feel stuck or like you're settling, and you know there is something more out there for you?

You're not alone.

Years ago, the Gallup organization began measuring the level of commitment employees felt toward their job and their employer. The numbers were startlingly low. Their research found that about one out of every five employees nationwide were truly excited about the work they were doing.

Over the years, these number have increased to an alarmingly high level. 80-90% of people say they are NOT happy at work.

Why have we settled for job misery?

PAUL STOLTZ GIVES US INSIGHT

Years ago, Oprah had a guest on her show that opened my eyes to what was happening in my life. His name was Paul Stoltz, author of *The Adversity Quotient*. According to Stolz, a person's Adversity Quotient (AQ) is the measure of *"one's ability to handle adversity."* Stolz says that if you don't have a high AQ, then you become easily overwhelmed and emotional, then pull back and stop trying.

In his book, Stolz states that people typically fall into one of three groups: **Quitters, Campers,** and **Climbers.**

1. **Quitters** are those people who have resigned from life and given up completely; they are bitter, depressed, and resentful. Campers are pretty much "retired Climbers" which means that they don't strive too hard or sacrifice as much as they once did.

2. **Campers** are only living 50% (or less) of their potential. They aren't really happy and they aren't too miserable either. They've found a tolerable place in life to "camp out" because on their way up the mountain they got tired and stopped.

3. Last, but not least, are the **Climbers**. Climbers are dedicated to constantly setting goals and achieving them. They make things happen, don't give up, learn from their mistakes, and move on. They are committed to a lifelong ascent up the mountain.

So, which one are YOU?

Quitters are at the bottom of the mountain, Campers are in the middle and the Climbers are at the top.

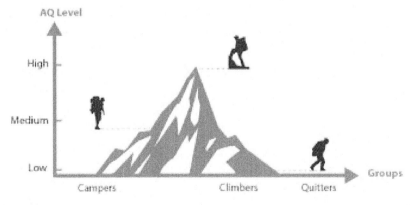

If you're reading this book, you're probably not a quitter. However, if you've stayed in a job you hate or that is unfulfilling for years, you might be a Camper.

Campers are living up to 50% of their potential. They don't have enough pain to change things, so they subconsciously camp out and accept the status quo.

We just suck it up and stay in a job we hate because it's a lot of work, energy, time, and risk to change it.

If you think you're in the Camper group, just know that you can decide right now to leave your campground (the status quo) and start climbing up the mountain.

IT ONLY TOOK ALEX ONE YEAR TO REALIZE HE WAS CAMPING

I recently hired one of my clients, 23-year-old Alex. He is a published author who has made almost $10,000 on the backend of his book, has started a successful podcast with over 5,000 subscribers, graduated from a top-tier college, and took a 6-figure job as a programmer/coder.

I happened to mention to him that I was looking for a project manager for my Bestselling Author business and he called me one day to see if I was still looking for help. I figured one of his classmates or friends needed a job. I was surprised to find out it was him.

I asked why he wanted to work for me when he had a successful 6-figure job at a big IT company, and he replied:

"This job was a great opportunity for me. But there is no way I'm going to sit in a cubicle for the rest of my life coding. I'm quitting my job to go travel the world."

I was in shock. It took me 17 years and getting fired to finally have the courage to go follow my dreams and here is this 23-year-old "kid" who figured it out in one year! Very inspiring.

Alex is a smart young adult who saved up a year's salary to go follow his dreams. He also lined up a few consulting gigs (like working for me) to supplement his income as he travels. He plans to visit several states and countries. He's even subleased his apartment for six months and then will let it go completely.

I'm proud of Alex for following his dreams and exploring the world. That's the best way to learn about who you are and what makes you happy.

You can't replace experience with reading about experiences. You have to go out and do it and then step back, assess the situation, and make the necessary shifts.

20 QUESTIONS THAT CAN CHANGE YOUR LIFE

To figure out what you want (and don't want) in your work and your life, answer these 20 questions to gain more clarity about your current job (and you can use it for past jobs as well).

Remember, it's important to know your history so you don't REPEAT IT.

Take the time to invest in yourself and answer ALL of the following questions.

You're worth it!

Get out your notebook and start answering the questions for your current job to start with and then you can go back later and do this for all of your jobs. Of course, if you're like me, you might need a second notebook!

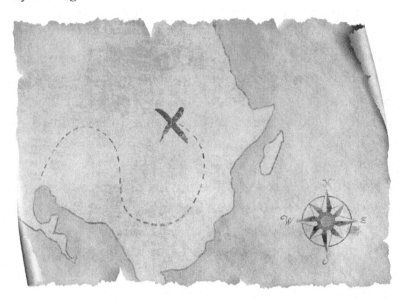

Job Autopsy Questions

1. Are you a people person or a project person? Which role do you play in your current job? Which do you prefer?

2. What duties (tasks) do you dislike and would give them to someone else if you could? What percentage of your day do you spend doing these things?

3. What duties (tasks) are you passionate about at work? What percentage of your day is spent doing these things?

4. Of all the jobs you've had in your life, which one did you love the most, and why?

5. If there was one change you could make at your current job to make you stay, what would that be and why?

6. What would your ideal/perfect workday look like? Provide details for hours, location, pay, tasks, vacation time, etc.

7. Do you feel respected at work?

8. Do you receive praise and recognition at work?

9. Do you like the hours of your job?

10. Do you like the location where you work?

11. What kind of expectations did you have when you first took this job?

12. What has been your biggest disappointment?

13. Do you like and respect your boss, or do you work for a jerk?

14. Do you have fun at your job?

15. Do you like your co-workers?

16. Are there any new skills you could learn that would improve your job? If so, what are they?

17. Do you think you should be making more money for what you do?

18. Is there room for advancement in your current position?

19. Is your work life and home life in balance? If not, what exactly is out of balance?

20. What would you miss the most if you quit your job?

By taking the time to answer these questions, you have gained more insight as to what the exact source of your unhappiness at work is.

This is important because it helps you to visually see where you went off course. Remember that *Career Creep* is a very slow, insidious process and most people don't even notice it happening until they are completely miserable.

I suggest answering the above questions for ALL of your past jobs as well as your current job as this will help you begin to see patterns and clues.

The next step is to assess your answers to the 20 questions because this will lead to deeper clarity.

THE CLUES ARE HIDDEN IN YOUR ANSWERS

People person vs. project person. The solution to this is pretty obvious. If you're a people person spending 90% of your day working at a computer, doing research, writing or working on big projects, you are going to be miserable at work, and vice versa. Is there a way to change this? Can you speak to your boss about changing some of your duties? Maybe you could make a lateral move within the company. Explore your options.

Duties you dislike. What percentage of your day is spent doing things you dislike? According to author Marcus Buckingham, "…successful people spend 75% or more doing what they like to do." So, if 75% or more of your day is spent doing what you don't like, you are not going to be happy or successful in the long-term. Determine if some of these tasks you dislike can be delegated to others within your department. There is a saying that there is no dirty work. This just means that there is always someone who loves to do what you hate doing and vice versa. Again, this requires talking to your boss and seeing if some of the tasks you dislike can be reassigned and delegated to others who actually like them.

Duties that you are passionate about at work. If you're not spending at least 75% of your day doing what you love, then you will feel emotionally, mentally and spiritually drained at the end of the day. The challenge here is to figure out how to do more of what you love at work. Maybe you can switch responsibilities with another employee?

Favorite Job. Was it your favorite job because you loved your boss, you had great co-workers, or because you truly loved the tasks you spent the majority of your time doing? Sometimes it's been so long that we've forgotten what once made us jump out of bed in the morning.

Changing One Thing at Work. What is the one thing you would change at work that would make you stay? Is it the pay, the hours, the boss, the team you work with? Is there a way to alter this one thing? If you don't like the location, perhaps you can transfer to another city or state. If you don't like the hours, maybe you could job share or work from home. If you don't like the salary, perhaps you can ask for a raise or a different position. If you are afraid to ask for what you want, then there is no possibility of ever getting it.

Your Perfect Workday. Writing out the details of your perfect day will give you clues to your heart's desire. The key is to let your imagination run wild and not modify what comes to your mind during this exercise. We all have that practical and realistic voice inside of our heads that will try to squelch anything that seems too far removed from our current situation. I want you to ignore that voice for this exercise. THINK ABOUT THIS: You can be *practical* or *magical,* but you can't be both for this exercise. Choose to be magical during this exercise and let your imagination run wild.

Respect. We don't usually pay any attention to it if we are getting it, however, if we're not getting respect, then we don't feel valued or important. Feeling respected is a basic human need we all have. If you don't feel respected at work, try brainstorming ways that might make you feel more valued. Talking to your boss is the first step in asking for what you need.

Praise and recognition. Another need we all share is a need for recognition. To deny this need is to deny your humanity. In my sales job years ago, the company I worked for recognized the top sales representatives at an annual awards banquet. Even though some people probably won't admit it, I think everyone appreciates the kudos and recognition we receive from the company we work for and from management. If you aren't getting the praise you need at work, you could make suggestions for contests and achievement awards. Again, don't be afraid to ask for what you want. Stop settling. You will never be content with less.

Job Hours. Some hours may seem set in stone, but often if we let our boss know we're not happy with them, we find out they're not set in stone. My best friend works four 10-hour days instead of five eight-hour days. Both my brother and my daughter-in-law work from home five days a week and they love it. When I was working in my sales job 20-25 hours per week, making six figures, I had lots of down time, which gave me the freedom to work on some of my passions – public speaking, teaching, writing, building an online business (that's why I labeled my outside sales job as my **FREEDOM JOB**). There are lots of creative ways to change your hours. The trick is to be able to explain to your employer how it will benefit them as well. Make it a win/win proposition.

Location. Sometimes there's not much you can do about the location unless the company has other locations that interest you. Research to see if there is another location that would suit you better. What would your ideal location be? Companies can save a lot of money by not having the overhead of office space; therefore, many companies now allow employees to work from home.

Expectations. Life is full of expectations and life is full of disappointments. Is it possible you had some unrealistic expectations when you took this job? If so, what were they? Why did you have those expectations? Were you living in fantasy land? By acknowledging what your expectations were, you can see where you have been let down. You may have to do a reset when it comes to these inaccurate expectations.

Biggest disappointment. Maybe you worked long and hard on a big project only to have your boss take all the credit. Yes, disappointments are part of life, but if we don't communicate our feelings to the person involved, we may be carrying around a lot of repressed *resentments*. Those resentments may be playing a big part in why you want to quit your job. We need to clean up this area, so we can be sure the exact reasons we want (or don't want) to quit our jobs. In a marriage, there are lots of disappointments, but it doesn't always mean divorce. Explore this area carefully and be honest with yourself.

Working for a Jerk. You may not like this advice, but I'm going to say it anyway – it's better for your peace of mind to *accept* that you work for a jerk than to think you can change a jerk. 99.9% of the time you CANNOT change jerks, however, you can change how you interact with them. *How do you do this*? Staying under the radar is one way; having minimal contact with that person is another. Get advice from others who seem to know how to handle this person. Tell the jerk how you feel about their behavior and ask for what you need. You could also try focusing on the jerks' good qualities. *What*? You say they have no good qualities. You may have to search far and wide, but I can assure you they have at least one redeeming quality. Don't quit your job because of a jerk. Jerks come and go – hopefully they'll move on. I almost quit my 6-figure sales job once because the company hired a "jerk" manager that I despised. I was talking to my sales team leader and he gave me great advice – *"Jerks come and go, just wait it out and he'll be gone before you know it."* So, I waited, and within six months, he was gone. Hallelujah! I kept my 6-figure cushy sales job.

Fun Factor. Is FUN missing from your work? Some types of work just don't seem to be much fun, but I think you can always inject some fun into the workplace if you try. I've worked at many law firms that had softball teams, Friday happy hours, and summer picnics on private islands. Initiate some of these activities if you like. When I was working for a law firm in DC, one of best days I remember was during the Christmas holidays when I brought homemade rum balls to the office. Everyone who ate the rum balls got quite a buzz – all before lunch! Food and drink always makes people lighten up; so do office toys like silly putty, character slippers, stress balls, yo-yos, and more. Get Creative!

Co-Workers. Sometimes people act one way at work and are completely different away from work (hopefully for the better). At least make an attempt to get to know your co-workers in other settings and environments; this may transform your relationship with them.

New Skills. Wouldn't it be a shame to get passed over for a promotion because you lacked a simple certification or training? This happens in a lot of companies. It may require time and effort on your part, but it will not only make you more marketable in the future, it can often get you more money. Years ago, a friend of mine was making $30,000 less than the going rate for her position in the Human Resources Department of a grocery store chain because she didn't have her

Master's degree. One day, she made the decision to go back to school part-time and get her Master's degree. It took her five years, but now she is making six figures. *What new skills can you learn at work*? When I worked for law firms, I took every free training course they offered, even if I wasn't currently using those specific skills or software in my job. I always knew down the road it would make me more marketable, would look great on my resume', and I might need those skills one day when I was finally able to quit my job. Remember, you may not always need these new skills right now, but if your company is paying for the training, I think it's worth investing your time to learn these new skills. SKILLS PAY THE BILLS!

Show me the Money. Of course, we all want to make more money, but sometimes we reach the top of the pay scale for a position. One of the many reasons I left the legal field was that I hit the top of the pay scale and there was nowhere else to go, except for the usual 2-3% annual salary increase. If you haven't reached the top, then it's time for you to ask for a raise. Before you do, make sure you come up with a valid list of reasons why you deserve a raise. Then ask.

Advancement. As a paralegal, I didn't have many options for traveling up the corporate ladder and getting a promotion unless I wanted to go back to school and get my law degree. Sometimes we can make lateral moves within the company.

Work and Home Life Balance. If your work life and home life are out of synch, it seems easy to blame it on your *big bad employer* who makes you work all those long hours for little pay. However, you agreed to it. Maybe it filled a void in your life, but now it is having negative consequences on you, your family, and maybe even your health. Implement new boundaries about what you are NOT willing to tolerate and get your life back in balance.

What would you miss if you didn't have your job? If you said "Nothing," then it's pretty clear that you absolutely need to quit your job. Most of us, however, can list a few things or people we would miss if we left. Making this list will help you gain perspective. Sometimes we think we want to quit our jobs when in reality, we just want to alter them a bit.

So how do you know when it's time to leave your job? Here are a few clues it's time to leave:

- ✓ You are absolutely burnt out in the industry.

- ✓ You spend 75% of your day doing tasks you hate, and there is absolutely no way to change this.

- ✓ You cannot be true to your soul in this job.

- ✓ Your skills are no longer necessary in your job.

- ✓ The nature of the job you are in does not align with your dreams.

- ✓ Your dreams can never be fulfilled while at this job.

- ✓ Your job is very stressful and is negatively affecting your health.

- ✓ Although you've tried to make changes, everything stays the same.

✓ Your core values are NOT in alignment with your employer's values.

Now that you've taken the time to do this transformative work and gain insight, you should have a sense of where you've been and how you ended up in your current job.

You may have discovered that by making some changes, you can tolerate your current job for a while, and create something you are passionate about on the side (a side hustle). Often, we can create something new on the side to get in a good financial place so we can quit our jobs permanently and do what we love!

Just know that YOU are responsible for your own workplace satisfaction, NOT your employer. To believe that your workplace is solely responsible for your happiness is to give your power away to your employer.

We take our power back when we take action and ask for what we need. If we don't get it, that's okay because then we can make a decision to leave or to stay. We are not victims unless we give our employers all our power and stay stuck in a job we hate for the rest of our lives.

Congratulations on doing the deep work! You dug deep into your job history and you have a better sense now of what is making you happy or unhappy when it comes to work.

Next, in Chapter 3, we are going soul searching instead of job searching...

MORE SOUL SEARCHING, LESS JOB SEARCHING

"A person doesn't know what he can do unless he tries. Trying things is the answer to finding your talent."

~Howard Finster
(Artist, who started painting at age 59)

The truth is most of us would rather go *job searching* than *soul searching*.

Why?

Because it's easier to skip soul searching and just go find another job; this way we don't have to ask ourselves the really hard questions like…

- **What brings me alive?**
- **What does my soul want to do?**
- **What brings me joy?**
- **What needs to die so my dreams can live?**

It is easier to live a *default* life than an *intentional* life.

After I left the law firm, I didn't know what I was going to do, but thankfully I was 100% certain I didn't want another job that left me feeling empty and unfulfilled.

Coming from the fast-paced legal environment, I was not accustomed to having downtime and I certainly didn't have time for soul searching. I had become comfortable with job misery. Intuitively, I knew I needed downtime to create my dream life, but I also felt guilty and stressed out for having so much free time when everyone in my life did not.

MEDITATION NOT MEDICATION

A couple of months after leaving the law firm, I experienced my first panic attack. I thought I was having a heart attack, so I asked a friend to take me to the emergency room. After extensive testing and an EKG, they determined that my heart was fine.

The doctor asked me if I had any stress in my life, to which I replied, *"No, I don't have any stress, everything is fine."*

I suppose because "high stress" was the norm in my life at the time, I didn't realize that all the changes were causing more stress.

THE MORE THE DOCTOR INQUIRED ABOUT MY LIFE, HERE'S WHAT HE DISCOVERED:

- **I was fired from my job at the law firm.**
- **I had no financial resources except a few months' severance pay.**
- **My ex-husband refused to pay child support, and I was constantly fighting with him to help me pay the bills and take care of the kids.**
- **My older brother and best friend was diagnosed with AIDS and was dying.**

- **The house I was renting was going to be sold, and I didn't have another place to move to since I had no job and no money in the bank.**
- **I didn't know what I was going to do with my life.**

The doctor determined that I did indeed have a lot of stress in my life, and he wanted me to see a psychiatrist. I had never been to a psychiatrist, so I took his advice and went to see one.

The psychiatrist he sent me to gave me a bad feeling right away. After a short conversation, he told me I was at high risk for suicide and that I needed to be on anti-depression medications right away.

I knew immediately this was not true.

I wasn't depressed, and I had never once thought about suicide. I realized he didn't know me, and he didn't know what he was talking about regardless of his degree and credentials on the wall in his office. Thankfully, I listened to my intuition and left his office as quickly as I could.

LISTEN TO YOUR OWN INTUITION

Doctors are not Gods. Unfortunately, many people treat them like they are. They are human beings with degrees and specialized training, but they don't have all the answers. If your gut is telling you something different, seek a second opinion.

Since I was a child, I have hated medications. I remember being five years old and my mother would try to give me over-the-counter medicine and I refused to take it. I felt that medicine was poison to my body. So when the doctor told me I needed to take this medicine (or I might die), I knew that was NOT what I needed.

I'm not suggesting or telling you to NOT take medicine you have been prescribed. However, for me, it was not the right option as I was not depressed or suicidal.

During the appointment, I even asked the psychiatrist what other options there were to medication and he said, *"There are none."*

I left his office and never returned. My instincts told me there was another option, so I headed to the bookstore to see what I could find.

I discovered a book called "Wherever You Go, There You Are" by Jon Kabat-Zinn which was about *meditation*. After doing some research, I discovered that there were many studies done about the physiological benefits of meditation including reducing anxiety and stress.

I DECIDED TO TRY MEDITATION INSTEAD OF MEDICATION

Meditation didn't work instantly, as I still was having panic attacks, but slowly over the next year, it worked. I never had another panic attack again.

It was challenging to get my mind to slow down and stop worrying and obsessing about the future. I started with two minutes a day and worked my way up to 20 minutes a day. As I began to practice meditation daily, my life changed drastically. I reconnected with my intuition and I started making more positive and informed choices from that place.

Positive choices like this led me to Unity Church which shifted my mindset and led me on a new spiritual path. I discovered the book "A Course in Miracles," which changed my life, and I began studying every self-help book I could get my hands on.

I also sought out a counselor (a Licensed Clinical Social Worker) to help me work on issues I had from my past. I loved therapy because it gave me so many new tools to use in my life that I did not have before. My therapist helped me remove the blinders and see things I wasn't aware of.

As I began to increase my faith, I took a 12-week class at Unity called the 4T Prosperity Course. During those 12 weeks, I had several financial windfalls come to me. I won't go into all the details, but I was beginning to have more faith and less worry.

I was still job-searching because it made me feel better studying the help wanted ads and submitting resumes, but the reality was that soul-searching was what I needed the most.

SOMETIMES WHEN WE'RE NOT SURE OF WHERE TO GO, WE HAVE TO GO BACKWARDS AND LOOK FOR CLUES

When I was a little girl, I loved to put on neighborhood shows. I would organize the *"entertainment"* which consisted of songs, skits, dances, and puppet shows. I loved being the center of attention. Ironically, the older I got, the more self-conscious I became until one day I woke up and I was the opposite of the center of attention; I was more like a wallflower. I kept to myself and only spoke to others if I was spoken to. It took me many years to get back in touch with this lost part of myself.

The longer we stay in a job or career we hate, the more removed we are from our innate joy, passion, and dreams until we can't even remember what they are. We literally have dream amnesia. Sometimes all we know is, *"I'm just not happy"* and *"There must be more to life than this."*

We may have material objects, we may even have cash, but on the inside is an empty feeling that whispers *there must be something more.*

Finding out exactly what that *something more* is the work we all must do if we are in a job that does not fulfill us. Finding what *you* need to feel fulfilled *is* work only you can do. The answers are inside of you.

Marcus Buckingham, author of the book *One Thing You Need to Know* says:

"Some people will tell you that it doesn't matter if you like your work; you just have to be good at it. Question this advice. You may well be good at some activities you don't enjoy, but your ENJOYMENT is the fuel you require to keep practicing the activity. Lacking this enjoyment, your performance will likely plateau."

Years ago, I met a man named Burt who mentored others in becoming professional speakers. Burt shared a personal story with me about how he had been a real estate guru for years earning *big dollars* in the real estate business. Thankfully, he realized one day that what he was really making was *empty dollars* because the real estate business did not *fulfill* him. Changing people's lives through speaking and being able to reach large groups of people is what Burt truly craved in his life. It gave his life meaning, and he decided that was more important to him than all the *empty dollars* in the world!

Once you are fully grounded in who you are – physically, emotionally, spiritually, and mentally – this knowingness will lead you to trust in your intuition and to follow your heart.

DON'T LISTEN TO THE WELL-MEANING ADVICE OF OTHERS

An ex-boyfriend of mine once asked me why I wanted to leave my *secure* job at the law firm to start my online business when I was already making *good money* with great benefits and was living a pretty comfortable life (according to him). He said I was living a life that most people only "dreamed about."

At first, I felt guilty for wanting something more and for not following the crowd. I thought to myself, "Maybe he's right, maybe I'm a bad person for wanting more. Maybe I should be happy with what I have when so many people have so much less than me."

Thankfully, I realized pretty quickly that my thinking was misguided.

OUR DESIRE FOR APPROVAL IS THE PATH AWAY FROM WHAT OUR SOUL CRAVES

When people we care about question something we are doing and that challenges the status quo, we pull back from our true desires because we want to fit in and we have a deep need for their approval. Our survival instincts (our primitive brain) tells us we need that approval or we will die. **This is NOT true.**

If you don't get approval from those closest to you, I can assure you that you won't die. It might feel like it though because you respect their opinions and it's scary to leave the "crowd," but the alternative is to lead a life of quiet desperation, and I don't think that's what you want or you wouldn't be reading this book. It isn't easy to go against what other people think is the right path for you, but the truth is, only your soul knows what the right path is for you.

LISTENING TO WHAT YOUR SOUL AND HEART WANTS WON'T ALWAYS BE THE POPULAR CHOICE

You have to be okay with not getting acceptance and approval from those closest to you. Keep your dreams to yourself and don't share them with others because many times those voices and opinions will deter you from making positive changes and taking a new path.

In her bestselling book, "The Artists Way," by Julia Cameron, she talks about *blocked friends* and *poisonous playmates*.

Blocked friends and poisonous playmates don't want us to change, to put ourselves first, to set aside time for play, daydream and do creative work or even to nurture ourselves. They want you to choose them and not yourself.

We often play nice and don't want to hurt other people's feelings which is why so many people default to giving their time and attention to others instead of themselves.

If you want to create a life you don't want to run away from, it's critical you become vigilant about where your time and energy goes, and also with whom you share your dreams and ideas.

Here are a few guidelines about sharing your dreams and ideas:

- **Make sure your friend or family member is nurturing and not toxic. No poisonous playmates here.**

- **Make sure your friend or family member is supportive of you and not jealous. No green-eyed monsters allowed.**

- **Make sure your friend is not a blocked creative and is pursuing their own dreams and goals. No blocked creatives here.**

- **Make sure your friend or family member is not a drama llama. You need peace, not drama, to create your dream life.**

Surround yourself with supportive people who want your highest good and are your biggest fans. Not everyone in your life will be that support system that you need, so make sure to protect your dreams and ideas from the non-supportive people.

Our small self wants to keep the status quo and not make waves. Of course, I didn't want to upset anyone when I left my legal job, but I had to do what was best for me.

I could have stayed in my legal job for the rest of my life and "settled" for a mediocre life that was unfulfilling, uninspiring, and unbearable; but deep down something was reassuring me that I deserved to be happy. At the end of the day, it didn't matter what other people thought I should be doing. What mattered is how I felt about what I was doing.

WHY IT'S BETTER TO WOBBLE THAN SETTLE

In the movie *The Wizard of Oz*, it took a tornado and an upside-down house to get Dorothy on the yellow brick road and back to her true home. When we are thousands of miles off our authentic path, sometimes it takes an act of God to wake us up from our deep sleep.

Getting fired from my job at the law firm felt like a life-changing tornado had entered my life, but it actually turned out to be exactly what I needed as it pushed me in the direction of my dreams. The day finally came when my need for security was overpowered by my desire for having a life on my own terms. The cost of that goal was "uncertainty."

We don't just snap our figures and have it all figured it. It's a process that takes time and I find most of the time we stumble into clarity.

Being open to learning and committed to growing is the key to finding that clarity in your life.

"Being yourself is not remaining where you are or being satisfied with what you are. It is the point of departure."

–Sydney J. Harris

There is something deep inside of you that feeds your soul. *Do you know what it is?*

I think a part of us knows what feeds our souls, but unfortunately, we've either ignored it, abandoned it, or simply forgotten whatever "*it*" is by making up excuses about how impractical, self-indulging or childish it would be to follow "it."

This is flawed thinking.

What Brings You Alive?

During one of our weekly sessions, my therapist said, "I don't know what it is Michelle, but when you were talking about writing, teaching, and your online business…it was like you were high on life."

I was on an adrenaline high because those topics (writing, speaking, my online business and creativity) are what feeds my soul. I get very excited and animated when I talk about these subjects. Her comment made me feel good because I knew how many years I didn't know what fed my soul and how far I traveled to get to this knowing place.

If you don't know what it is that feeds your soul, some of the exercises in this book will point you to new directions to explore. Think of it as a trip down the yellow brick road that will eventually lead you back home!

In order to discover what feeds your soul, it is important to:

- **Create a written mission statement to help clarify your goals.**
- **Know your strengths.**
- **Recognize your demons.**
- **Be honest about what you enjoy doing and especially what you DON'T enjoy doing.**
- **Have a purpose for what you will be doing.**

A MISSION STATEMENT WILL HELP YOU LEARN TO SAY NO

A mission statement is a written statement of your purpose and reason for being.

I highly recommend the book, "The Path: Creating Your Mission Statement for Work and for Life" written by Laurie Beth Jones. Years ago, I taught a class at Unity, and it helped me and my students get more clarity in our lives.

Laurie Beth Jones has created a very easy formula for writing your mission statement. First, she suggests that you choose three verbs that excite you because every mission must have "action"; then, choose your core values (what you stand for) and the group or cause which most moves you (who you came here to help). A+B+C=D

I wrote the following mission statement years before I left my job at the law firm and long before I was following my dreams:

"My mission is to inspire, educate and motivate others to believe in themselves and to find their true purpose in life."

Once I had a written mission statement, new "opportunities" came along to test me to see if I was focused and committed. Reading and re-reading my mission statement helped me to say NO when new opportunities came along that didn't move me closer to my mission.

Having your own written mission statement will get you more focused so you're not living a life of default but living a life of design.

If you are bored, restless, and hate your job, these are all signs that you are **NOT** living your life on purpose. As I said, first you must discover who *you* are before *you* get the answer to what your purpose is.

TREASURE MAP EXERCISE: SOUL SEARCHING

STEP 1: Make a list of your 10 favorite activities that bring you the most JOY (enJOYment). (*Examples*: Sitting at the Ocean; Writing; Decorating; Baking; Organizing; Storytelling; Burning Candles; Running; Painting). If you get stuck, think about activities you engage in where you lose all sense of time. *Even if you haven't done these activities for a while (months or years), write them down. *Don't think about how to make money with these activities, just write 10 things that bring you JOY.

"It is in his pleasure that a man really lives... It is from his leisure that he constructs the true fabric of self."

~Agnes Repplier, an American Essayist

STEP 2: Now, choose two of these JOYful activities you would like to earn money doing.

For example, I love sitting at the ocean and I love writing. Years ago, I was cleaning out my closet when I stumbled upon some old journals written during various vacations to the beach when my kids were younger. I began reading them and thought to myself, *"This writing is really good. I can't believe I wrote this. My writing is so different (better...deeper...more alive) when I'm at the ocean than when I'm at home."*

Then, at that exact moment in time, I turned the TV on to "Good Morning America" and saw William Haley being interviewed about his father, Alex Haley. Alex Haley wrote the bestselling book *Roots* that sold over one million copies in the first year and was turned into a miniseries that was watched by an astonishing 130 million people. *Roots* also won both the Pulitzer Prize and the National Book Award. In the interview, William Haley was sharing that his father said he did his best writing when he was near the water. Alex Haley would often hop on board a freight or cargo ship and take long trips to do his writing. The crux of the story was that whenever his dad needed to write he made sure he was near the water because it got his creative juices flowing.

After seeing this interview, I had an "aha" moment. I decided to offer a class called "Ocean Writing" and through a series of synchronistic events and listening to my heart www.OceanWriting.com was born!

I combined my two passions – "writing" and "being at the ocean" – and created a very successful writers' program that I teach annually. Pretty cool that I created a way to get paid to sit at the ocean, huh?

Now that I've given you an example of how to get your creative juices going, what two Joys from your list above can you combine to come up with a unique business?

During one of my workshops, I had a woman in my class who combined the stock market with horoscopes and created several business ideas like a board game based on the financial tendencies of particular horoscope signs. Brilliant!

The point is to think outside the box.

If you want to find work that feels like PLAY, you do have to PLAY.

STEP 3: List two or three combinations of things that bring you JOY from your list above to come up with a unique business. (REMEMBER: Have FUN with these exercises. Play with your imagination and give yourself the gift of exploring without any commitment).

Let me give you an example of a real business that combines two unrelated passions...

I was watching "Cupcake Wars" when I saw two young entrepreneurs who started a bakery in Las Vegas called, "**Showboy Bake Shop**" where they combined their love of show business and good cake!

The owners, Stephen Lowry and Jared Sullivan's, had a background in stage, film and design. They also both loved baking.

Can you see how powerful it is to take two of your passions and come up with a unique business?

STEP 4: List your favorite combination of these two activities that can be a unique business.

STEP 5: Pick your favorite way of providing a service to others from the list above.

STEP 6: List 10 specific action steps you can do now to take this idea to implementation.

Remember: We are just imagining and playing to see what shows up—there are no right or wrong answers.

Nine Lives Game

You've probably heard that cats have nine lives. Perhaps that is why cats are so laid back and calm. They know when their current life ends, they're coming back again. For a moment, let's pretend that you have nine lives, too.

STEP 1: If you had nine lives and could be nine different people—what would you be? Examples: Writer, Gourmet Chef, Professor, Race Car Driver, Athlete, Mayor, Chocolatier. Don't use your logical mind; use your creative mind and give yourself permission to dream!

Barbara Sher, author of *I Could Do Anything if I Only Knew What It Was* (excellent book that I highly recommend) says we've been trained to **believe that we only get one choice in our lives.** This isn't true at all. We have an endless amount of choices; so, what we really need to **learn is how to manage these choices.**

Once you have chosen your nine lives, then answer the questions below which will help you manage your choices better. The point is, we can't do everything all at once, but if we manage our time better, we can do a lot more than we are doing right now.

STEP 2: Review your list, then answer these questions:

- **Which of the nine lives above can you focus on this year?**
- **When that one is complete, which one can you focus on next year?**
- **Which of the nine lives can you focus on for 30 minutes to an hour each day?**
- **Which one can you do on occasion?**

STEP 3: Make a 3-year JOY plan. Which JOYs can you focus on each year?

Strengths And Talents Finder

Often, when we are good at something – when it comes natural to us and doesn't require effort – we don't think of it as our strength because we take it for granted. Sometimes, we mistakenly believe that everyone can do this particular skill.

Writing has been one of those skills that I took for granted for a long time. I thought everyone could write and that everyone enjoyed writing. I found out that was not true.

The exercise below is a skill assessment to put your strengths and talents on paper so you can look at them more objectively. Usually people see traits in us that we don't see in ourselves.

Many years ago, I joined Toastmasters to overcome my fear of public speaking. Other members would tell me after I gave a speech how "great" my talk was and how "confident" I was when I spoke.

At the time, I had a tremendous amount of fear and couldn't understand what these people were talking about. In fact, I thought they were all crazy! They were seeing something in me that I wasn't able to see in myself.

Sometimes we are blind to our own talents. That's why we need other people to help us see our blind spots.

STEP 1: Write five skills you use in your current job that you like:

STEP 2: Write five skills people say you are good at:

STEP 3: Write two skills you enJOY the most from both of the above lists:

STEP 4: List 10 businesses you could start using these two skills:

Richard Bode, author of *Beachcombing at Miramar* says:

It astounds me when I think of the courage it takes to live, to behave as we want to behave, to be who we want to be. The world is filled with those who would keep us from singing the songs we want to sing, painting the pictures we want to paint, skimming the stones we want to skim. Some are bosses, some are officials of oppressive regimes – and some are our mothers, fathers, teachers, husbands, or wives, who for whatever reasons, try to stifle the life force that makes us who we are. But we have this choice: We can empower them or we can empower ourselves.

That is a powerful statement. Bode was a middle-aged man who left an unhappy marriage and a long career with a NY public relations agency giving up a chance to become a millionaire in order to live a more authentic life. Although when others mentioned to Bode how courageous they felt he was by leaving his highly successful job, Bode says, *"I can no more say I acted with courage when I quit that job than I can say a man who is suffocating acts with courage when he tries to breathe."*

Bode quit his job, sold his belongings, placed his cash in a shoe box, and became a "beachcomber" to seek the truth about his life – that was his dream. He wrote two books about what he discovered through this process, which I absolutely love! Both books are inspiring and motivating – which we all need daily doses of.

Quitting Your Job and Following Your Dreams is not an easy path – although others may see it that way. Bode says that many people think that being a beachcomber is "the easiest job in the world." He disagrees and explains in his book that being a beachcomber is a demanding job that calls for *discipline* and *zeal*.

NEWS ALERT! So does the path you have ventured onto.

Now it's time to look at our shadow side that may be sabotaging our dreams...

MAKE FRIENDS WITH YOUR DEMONS OR ELSE

Pia Melody, author of *Facing Codependence* says you have to, "Hug your demons or they will bite you in the ass."

If you don't embrace what is dysfunctional in you, then you are doomed to repeat it and stay in the past. Notice she didn't say "change," she said "embrace." There is a big difference.

What demons have you been ignoring that are holding you back from your dreams?

In her book, *The Dark Side of the Light Chasers*, author, Debbie Ford explains how important it is to our personal growth to "unmask those aspects of ourselves, which destroys our relationships, kills our spirit and keeps us from fulfilling our dreams."

Carl Jung, noted psychologist, said the shadow is those parts of ourselves we try to hide and deny.

"What we don't own, owns us."

So, what are some common shadows we try to hide, deny, or repress?

- **Fear**
- **Greed**
- **Ugliness**
- **Impatience**
- **Being Manipulative**
- **Being Disorganized**
- **Being Judgmental**
- **Anger**
- **Emotional problems**
- **Laziness**
- **Selfishness**

In our wholeness, we possess both sides of each trait which means that you are at times both strong and weak; patient and impatient; generous and greedy. When any of these traits are not balanced and in check, they can be blocks that prevent us from living our dreams.

Balancing our shadow selves by fully owning them will help clear the path to your dreams.

If you do not feel worthy of living your dreams, or having the desires of your heart, then there is an internal block that needs to be addressed. If this is an area in which you need help, then I recommend reading Debbie Ford's book mentioned above and spending time with a good therapist or counselor that can help you work on those parts of yourself that you are rejecting.

Nathaniel Brandon, author of many amazing books on self-esteem, says:

> *"Productive achievement is a consequence and an expression of healthy self-esteem, not its cause..."*

In order to self-realize your dreams, it's important to feel good about who you are because when you do, your *daily behaviors* will be in line with those feelings.

Your daily behaviors either contribute or take away from your goals and dreams.

Write It Down If You Expect It To Ever Happen

Once you begin to get clarity about your future dreams and aspirations, it is imperative that you write them down. Henriette Anne Klauser, author of *Write it Down, Make it Happen,* says:

> *"Writing down your dreams and aspirations is like hanging up a sign that says, Open for Business."*

We have lots of thoughts running through our minds daily. In fact, according to the National Science Foundation, the average person thinks an average of 1,000 thoughts per hour and has approximately 12,000 thoughts per day. Some statistics are even higher. The thoughts that are repeated are what mold and shape our lives.

This is extremely important.

The successful people in life choose the same thoughts daily, and those thoughts are positive, uplifting and constructive.

So not only do we have to become more aware of the thoughts we have every day, but when we want to create something new in our life, we need to send out a signal to the universe about our dreams – writing down your dreams and goals will begin the process of attracting the people and circumstances needed for you to achieve those dreams and goals.

A Course in Miracles says:

"The moment you set an intention, the Universe conspires to assist you."

It is comforting to know you are not alone; you are being guided and supported. I strongly believe if you have the desire in your heart, then you also have the abilities and capabilities within you to make those desires a reality.

MY DESIRE TO MAKE 6 FIGURES DROVE ME

Working as an outside sales representative in an all-commission job selling hot tubs, I earned $60K the first year which was the "average" for salespeople in the company. Within 18 months of joining the company, however, I was able to double my income! Other sales reps in the company wanted to know my "secret" to making a six-figure income and doubling my income.

The secret is this: I *tracked* my income weekly. In the past, I used to keep careful *track* of my bills and guess what? My bills grew bigger and bigger. This time, I *tracked* my income in an Excel spreadsheet that I would print every time I had a sale. I had a yearly goal to make six figures, and within 18 months, I achieved that goal!

What you "focus" on grows. Just like plants need water to grow; your dreams need daily focus in order to grow, too.

ORGANIZING YOUR LIFE AND YOUR GOALS

In his book, *The 26-Hour Day* by Vince Panella, a time-management expert, the author advises that there is no such thing as time management until you write down where you are now in your life and where you want to be in six months. Do this for every area of your life such as:

- **Health**
- **Finances**
- **Family**
- **Relationships**
- **Spirituality**
- **Travel**
- **Home**
- **Business**

Then, transfer the information from your notes on to index cards that you read each morning when you wake up. The idea is that it puts your goals in the forefront of your mind each day and your to-do list is based on these written down goals. Without the goal-setting exercise, your to-do list is pretty much worthless.

I have done the exercises in his book and they work! After doing this for six months, I achieved many of the goals I wrote down on the note cards. Then, I reviewed the cards and created new ones for the next six months. My to-do list is based on my goals and that is what moves me closer and closer to reaching my goals every day. I do this every six months.

Make your TO-DO list based on your goals.

HOW CATTLE RANCHERS MOVE CATTLE

I recently heard a story about a cattle rancher who had to move large herds of cattle from one location to the next. This was before they had fences, so there was nothing to contain the cattle. He said that the cattle would go way off course so to bring them back, they would tie a donkey's leg to the leg of the cattle. The cattle would try to break free from the donkey by jerking around. Every time the cattle did this, the donkey would move one step closer to home.

The donkey had something the cattle did not. **Intention**. The donkey wanted to return home because the donkey knew where the food and water was. So, one step at a time, the donkey would bring home cattle that were miles off course.

The moral of the story is that even if you take one small step per day towards your goals, at the end of the year, you will be 365 steps closer to achieving your goals. Nothing is impossible; only the limitations you create in your mind.

The other side of the coin is: It's NOT easy! If it was easy, everyone would be living their dreams instead of a 90% job dissatisfaction rate!

If you don't give up, you will achieve much more than if you never try.

STOP! Write down the goals you want to achieve in the next six months. Do not read anymore until you have your goals in black and white in front of you. Tell the Universe what you want! Include the following areas of where you are now and where you want to be:

- Health
- Finances
- Family
- Relationships
- Spirituality
- Travel
- Home
- Business

Your RAS Is Helping You Sort It All Out.

Did you know there is a system inside of you to help you attract what you want?

It would be impossible to sort and process all of the information available to us. The good news is that in your brain is something called a *Reticular Activating System* (RAS) to help you with all of this. An RAS is basically your own personal assistant who will bring "relevant" information to your attention. So, what is "relevant" information?

Let's say you are at a football stadium watching a game with thousands of other fans. There is a lot of noise from the fans cheering, people talking, announcements, and music. Suddenly, a voice over the loudspeaker calls your name and your attention is on full alert. Your RAS has been activated. Your RAS acts on your behalf as a filter to bring to your attention *relevant information* and helps you leave behind the rest. By repeating thoughts daily and writing down your dreams and goals, you are providing your RAS something to work with.

Several years ago, I was on a conference call with Jack Canfield, co-author of the *Chicken Soup for the Soul* series. During this call, Jack mentioned how important it was to be vividly clear about what you wanted and to write it down because he said this is what *"PROGRAMS YOUR UNCONSCIOUS."*

Let's say you have a goal along with an affirmation that says, "I want to own a Lexus." Since the reality is that you don't currently own a Lexus, according to Canfield, a *structural tension* is created in your brain. The brain always wants to resolve any structural tension. In order to do that, you will begin to draw to you what is needed to achieve the goal, which will in turn, resolve the structural tension.

That's why this book has lots of exercises for you to write your answers down so it brings those ideas to the front and center of your attention. **Writing down your goals is key!**

Soul searching is NOT a one and done event. It's a life-long process.

We are always changing and evolving. Just like in nature, nothing stays the same. We are either dying or growing.

Our goal is to evolve and become a climber, not a camper. When we make positive choices that are led by our souls, then we create a life we don't want to run away from. That's why taking the time to do the exercises in this book and soul searching is such an important part of the process. It's about getting to know yourself again.

Now it's time to take some of your answers in this chapter and start testing things out with fun action and activities...

CHAPTER 4

VOCATION VACATIONS

"The secret to success is to make your Vocation a Vacation."

~Mark Twain

This chapter is all about test driving some of your vocation options before you go all in.

After my son Jason graduated from high school, like many people, he was trying to figure out what he wanted to do with the rest of his life. One day after visiting the local college, he became interested in massage therapy. He looked at the curriculum and decided *100%, without a doubt,* he wanted to become a massage therapist.

I was about to invest $10,000+ for the program when the thought popped into my head that I should take him to talk to a friend of mine who was a massage therapist. This way, he could get a massage, talk to her about the business side of things, and then decide if this was something he really wanted to do. I guess my gut was telling me that we needed to be 100% certain this was the right path for my son so we both didn't waste a lot of time and money.

The day before Jason was supposed to enroll in the massage therapy program, I took him to my friend's house where he received a full body massage and then he asked the massage therapist questions about the business. I was so excited as we left her house because it seemed to me that things went well.

As we left her house, I asked my son what he thought about everything and was quite surprised when he replied, "I could never be a massage therapist. I could never do that to strangers!" I was so thankful I made that decision and did not invest $10,000 in tuition only to find out down the road my son really wasn't happy with that choice.

FAST FORWARD TO TODAY

Today, my son has found his passion in sales. He is one of the top sales professionals at Lexus and recently won the *Presidential Award*! Every year, he earns bonuses and they send him on a trip to Mexico. My son is super smart and super successful – he makes six figures, owns his own home (which will be paid off in seven years), owns a brand-new Sea Ray boat, and is married to the love of his life. I'm also happy to report that he absolutely loves what he does for a living. Imagine if he had gone through the massage therapy school and then felt guilty because of the money I invested on the tuition and stayed with that job for the wrong reasons. He would have been miserable to say the least.

This is becoming more and more common – people go to college or university to get a degree, only to find out **AFTER** graduation that they don't like their chosen field. They end up staying in jobs for years and decades because of the money they invested in their education and the student loans they have to pay back.

LAWYER TURNED WINDOW SALESPERSON

Another example of someone in the wrong career is my former attorney who absolutely hated practicing law but was extremely good at it. He handled a case for me years ago, and I can honestly say, I've never seen a better trial lawyer. We won a very difficult case. However, as a practicing attorney, he was miserable.

As fate would have it, a series of unfortunate events happened that caused him to lose his license to practice law. Or maybe these weren't unfortunate events but synchronistic events, designed to bring him back to his authentic path. The great news is he's now a top sales representative for a well-known window company, and he loves it. He told me that he's much happier selling windows than he ever was practicing law.

This is why I like the idea of "test driving" your dream job. I know now that's what I was doing in my younger days by taking a variety of jobs and trying them out for a while. I was just "test driving" jobs to see what I liked.

JUST FOR LAUGHS, HERE ARE A FEW OF THE JOBS I SAMPLED:

- **WWF Wrestling Girl** – Yes, that's right! I used to walk up the WWF wrestlers in the 1980s! I walked up a guy by the name of "Playboy Buddy Rose" and hung out with well-known wrestlers like Andre the Giant, Mr. Perfect, Bob Backlund, and other wrestling celebrities at the time.

- **Cocktail Waitress** – This was such a fun job! I met a lot of celebrities who stayed at this Sheraton Hotel during my time there. I also worked at the J.W. Marriott Hotel in D.C. and that was fun as well.

- **Private Process Server** – This was an interesting job serving people who were evading service. I became quite good at figuring out creative ways to get people served. One time, I went to a bar where the defendant was hanging out and I had the papers I was serving wrapped in a Christmas gift box. I pretended to give him a Christmas present and got him served. At the time, I only had to touch his body with the papers. He could tear them up, throw them away, or walk away from them, but he was served.

- **Jewelry Store Salesperson** - I hated this job because I hated retail and I couldn't stand waiting around for people to come into the store.

- **Cashier at McDonald's** – This was my first job at age 15½ and I had fun working there with my older brother, Michael.

- **HVAC sales rep** – I knew nothing about HVAC, but they convinced me I could sell their products, and they were wrong. I didn't have the knowledge required to sell this product and I wasn't good at climbing ladders and going on top of tall buildings.

- **Real Estate Magazine Presenter** – I travelled around to various real estate offices and sold advertising space in an industry magazine. It was fun for a while, but not enough pay.

- **Freelance Instructor for Community Colleges** – As a sub-contractor for the College, I was sent to various locations to teach business writing. I really wanted to teach creative writing and public speaking. It paid the bills, but I didn't enjoy it.

- **Newspaper Reporter** – I mentioned this job earlier. I loved chasing and writing stories, but I didn't love the pay. It served its purpose and got me the writing credentials I needed to do other things.

- I had many more jobs! These were just a few.

When I was a serial job hopper, everyone around me thought I was crazy. My ex one time called me a "Job Whore" because I had 2-3 jobs at a time and was always changing jobs.

I suppose I looked very unstable; constantly changing jobs, however, without trying out jobs, I really didn't know what I liked and didn't like. They seemed like good jobs, but you never know until you actually work in a job if you will enjoy it or not.

I guess it's kind of like dating. The point of dating is to see if you want to be with that person long term. I was just dating jobs instead of people!

PIVOT PLANET TO THE RESCUE

Luckily for you, there is a company, *Pivot Planet* (**www.pivotplanet.com**) that can arrange for you to "test drive" your dream job or dream business. After all, it would be a great misfortune to quit your job only to find out down the road that you really didn't like what you thought was going to be your *dream* job or *dream* business.

Career coaching is a popular way to help you figure out what direction to take. That is a great idea, however, I like the concept of working with Pivot Planet that provides virtual mentorship with real people in real careers. Here is an excerpt from their website:

- Since 2004, Pivot Planet's founder, Brian Kurth, and his Vocation Vacations career mentorship team have provided thousands of one to three-day in-person mentorship experiences to people exploring a new career or a path not taken.

- For as little as $50 per hour, Pivot Planet connects people around the world looking to "pivot" from an existing career to a new career or enhance their current job skills with expert advisors working in hundreds of fields. These advisors offer affordable, one-on-one video and phone sessions. Pivot Planet also offers the option of in-person mentorship with some of its advisors.

- Pivot Planet goes beyond connecting online, career coaching or corporate outplacement.

- Pivot Planet is the resource for finding real-life career and start-up business advice shared by experienced advisors who can answer your questions and offer insights into their profession. Anywhere. Anytime."

I love it! I wish this program had been around when I was in my 20's! It would have saved me from taking a lot of jobs I ended up hating.

Hobby or Jobby?

Remember what Elizabeth Gilbert said about blending hobbies with jobs. Sometimes the two should not be blended.

My friends and family always comment how great I am at cooking and baking. Many people have suggested that I start my own catering business, but I know myself well enough to know that I enjoy cooking on a small scale (as a hobby) and that I would never be happy spending eight or more hours a day in a hot kitchen doing prep work and cooking for large parties or as a job. I know without a doubt that cooking is just my hobby.

Often, there is a fine line between a hobby and a vocation.

Sometimes we ruin our hobbies by trying to turn them into businesses.

It's not a mistake to try, but don't invest too much into it. My rule of thumb is go and make your first $100 doing whatever "it" is and then reassess that decision and see if you actually enjoyed the experience before you take a deep dive into it.

I've known many people over the years who say they want to have an online business, but they really hate being at the computer and despise technology. Therefore, it wouldn't be a good fit, and they would be miserable having an online business.

I've also met people who say they want to write books, but when it comes to actually writing the book, they don't like the process of sitting down to the blank page and doing the actual writing.

It doesn't mean you can't start an online business or write a book if you hate the process; you can absolutely outsource the parts of the business you're not good at. For example, many of my authors use ghostwriters to get their book written.

It's important to look at the difference between a hobby and a dream job. Our dream job (or business) should involve things we enjoy doing that may (or may not) be hobbies, and our hobbies may be things we can make money at.

So, how do we know if we should make our hobby our dream job?

Well, one way would be to test it out.

Get a part-time job before leaving your full-time job to see if you really like it. You could also volunteer at an organization where you would like to work.

If your dream job is working for yourself, find someone else who is doing something similar to what you want to do and ask them if you can work for them as an intern to see if it really is your dream job.

I encourage you to "test drive" your dream job or hobby-based job with **Pivot Planet** as part of your exploration for the next chapter in your life. Some of the advisors they have (and there are hundreds are):

- Travel Writer
- Chief Technology Officer
- Actor
- Dog Daycare Owner
- Digital Strategist
- Make-up Artist
- Magazine Editor

- Distiller
- Music Producer
- Filmmaker
- Fitness Trainer
- Non-profit Director
- Home Stager
- Pet Resort Owner
- Pastry Chef
- Pastor
- Publisher
- Psychologist
- Professional Poker Player
- Private Investigator
- Wine Tasting Room Owner

And the list goes on and on! Check it out yourself: **https://www.pivotplanet.com/browse**

This is a great way to try out your ideas before taking the plunge!

Find creative ways to try out your dream jobs (or businesses) using some of the things you listed in Chapter 3 (Remember: Go Soul Searching NOT Job Searching).

Maybe you thought you really wanted to be a veterinarian, but after trying it out, you discovered you really want to be an animal trainer. Or perhaps you thought you loved organizing people's closets only to discover you'd rather organize their finances.

Go where your excitement is, however, also make a mental note that every hobby that excites you (or everything you are curious about) is NOT automatically going to be your dream job or dream business! Sometimes what we do for a few hours a month as a hobby would make us crazy if we had to do it eight hours a day as a job.

Explore your choices by trying them out *before* making a final decision.

Pivot Planet Founder Brian Kurth says:

"Think of it as a risk-free way of sampling your dream without quitting your day job. It's a taste that gives you a chance to determine... do I want to pursue this?"

WHAT'S YOUR FANTASY?

Go back to Chapter 3 and review your answers to the Nine Lives Game (*If you had nine lives and could be nine different people – what would you be?*). After reviewing your list, I want you to write your top three choices below. These should be the ones that get your juices flowing!

MY TOP 3 LIVES FROM THE 9 LIVES GAME ARE:

1. _____
2. _____
3. _____

CHOOSE ONE OF THE THREE LIVES TO FOCUS ON.

Write what your perfect day would look like if you were living this life.

Write the details in your journal! Here are some details you might think about:

- **Where you are living?**
- **What time of day or night do you work?**
- **Do you work from home?**
- **Do you travel?**
- **Who is around you?**
- **Who works for you?**
- **How do you spend your day?**
- **How much money do you get paid?**
- **How do you get paid?**
- **Who are your dream clients?**

Remember, our dreams and visions are first created in our mind's eye. This is a safe place for you to explore your fantasies. Sometimes as adults, we forget how to *daydream*. To create a life we truly love, we must re-learn the forgotten art of daydreaming and fantasies, and most importantly, we must be SPECIFIC.

Fairy Tales Help Us Learn About Who We Are

Most of us heard some or all of these Fairy Tales:

- Little Red Riding Hood
- Cinderella
- Sleeping Beauty
- Snow White
- Hansel and Gretel

The common denominator in these fairy tales is that they all have lots of obstacles and happy endings, right?

Fairy tales are important because they speak to our subconscious. They remind us to ask questions, to never give up in our quest for happiness, to retain the wonderment of childhood, to utilize our imagination, and that dreams can, and do, come true.

Fairy tales also help us dig deep within ourselves to discover new things about ourselves, how to overcome problems (even seemingly impossible ones), and they tell us that if we follow the right path, then our dreams can come true.

In the book, *Modern Fantasy: Children's Literature, Discovery for a Lifetime* by Barbara D. Stoodt-Hill and Linda B. Amspaugh-Corson (Prentice-Hall, 1996) the definition of fantasy is:

"...fantasy always includes at least one element of the impossible, one element that goes against the laws of the physical universe, as we currently understand them; it concerns things that cannot really happen, people or creatures that do not really exist. Nevertheless, each story must have its own self-contained logic that creates its own reality."

You can choose to be practical or magical, and it's time for you to be magical!

The book goes on to say:

"Fairy tales are unbelievable stories featuring magic and the supernatural. Fairies, giants, witches, dwarves, good people, and bad people in fairy tales live in supernatural worlds with enchanted toadstools and crystal lakes. Heroes and heroines in these stories have supernatural assistance in solving problems."

Although the fairy tale may have a happy ending, usually obstacles arise somewhere in the middle of the plot. There is the "impossible" element that must be acknowledged.

Don't deceive yourself by seeing only the "good part" of your dream job or business. Fairy tales are designed to mirror real life struggles.

Don't delude yourself, because the truth is …

There is no perfect job or business.

As human beings, no matter what role we are in, we have both weaknesses and strengths. Fairy tales help us see the positive as well as the negative. They help us see the dark and the light. This is extremely important or else there is a good chance we might delude ourselves into seeing only the good without seeing the obstacles and struggles that we are sure to encounter as we move towards our dreams. It's important to name our potential obstacles.

NAME 3 POTENTIAL OBSTACLES YOU MIGHT FACE IN YOUR DREAM JOB OR BUSINESS:

1. _____
2. _____
3. _____

PLAY OUT THESE 3 OBSTACLES IN YOUR MIND AND ON PAPER IN GREAT DETAIL

What would be the parts of your dream job that you really don't like?

Understand that there is never going to be a job or a business that you love doing 100% of the tasks. If you spend at least 75% of your time doing what you love, you will be happy and joyous.

Write down below at least three things you don't like about your dream job/business. Be brutally honest with yourself.

WRITE DOWN 3 THINGS YOU KNOW YOU WON'T LIKE ABOUT YOUR DREAM JOB/BUSINESS:

1. _____
2. _____
3. _____

If you talk to others who are in the line of work you are considering, or if you hire an advisor on **Pivot Planet**, make sure you ask them what part(s) of their jobs they don't like.

MY FRIEND QUIT THE SAME JOB THREE TIMES

My good friend, Jenny, was in mortgage banking for many years and loved the part of her job that involved doing the numbers, taking loan applications, finding the right loans for people, but she *HATED* the part of the job that involved having to go out in the field to sell the product. Even though she was good at "sales," she intensely hated "cold calling." Jenny explains that lots of people go into this type of business—mortgage banking, then face the fierce competition and rejection and become dismayed. Jenny got in and out of mortgage banking three different times because she says, "the money was so good."

The first time Jenny quit mortgage banking, she got a job as a waitress, then did some temp work, and decided to go back into mortgage banking because she knew the money was there. The second time she quit mortgage banking, she sold the home she owned and was living on her equity. When the money ran out, she went back into mortgage banking again because she got a great offer she couldn't turn down. Inside though, she was miserable.

She left once again and got a job as a secretary. Again, being lured by the money, she went back into the mortgage business one final time. That third and last time, she knew she would never return because she finally acknowledged to herself that being in the mortgage banking was:

"Like sandpaper rubbing against my soul."

Jenny finally realized that the money she was earning was not worth selling her soul!

Jenny reminds us:

"People get stuck in the money part, and in chasing the money. Yes, we need money to survive, but you can't put a dollar figure on the JOY in your heart. You become rich in your soul when you do what you love and nobody can take that away."

The next step in this journey is clearing out the old to make room for the NEW...

PART II - CLEARING

---

*"The wisdom of life consists in
the elimination of non-essentials."*

~ Lin Yutang

CHAPTER 5

IT TAKES AN INTERMISSION
TO FIND YOUR MISSION

Tama Kieves, author of *This Time I Dance! Trusting the Journey of Creating the Work You Love,* said this after taking a 10-day vacation at a beach away from her high stress job as an attorney:

> **"I could not assess my job and my life while in the thick of the job that was my life."**

You must find a way to remove yourself, if only for a few days, from the job that drains your energy and dampens your spirits and go to a space where you can rest, reflect, revamp, and reconnect to what you truly want your life to be.

If you can get to a faraway beach or the mountains, that's great; but if you can only get to the local park that has a lake and a bench under a shaded tree, then by all means, go for it! Tama suggests:

> **"Consciously let go of what tires you.
> And what inspires you will take its place."**

Where you go to rest isn't as important as just stepping out of your life for a few hours or a few days (or more if you can) to regain a fresh perspective. It's amazing when I go on vacation or away for a girl's only weekend, how I am able to have a different view of my life and business.

After I left the legal field, I was fortunate to find a job doing outside sales (my **FREEDOM JOB**) that was much more aligned with who I was. It gave me a lot of free time to follow my curiosities, get back to daydreaming, and allowed me to use my imagination and recharge. I was blessed because I only worked 20-25 hours a week doing outside sales and was making six figures; it gave me the freedom I craved because my bosses were 350 miles away from me; and most importantly, it gave me the space I needed to start exploring my buried dreams.

I've learned that the longer you spend disconnected from your passions and your true self, the longer it takes you to reconnect and recover. There's a lot of rest time, sleep time, and time-outs needed!

The outside sales job I had, with its minimal hours and high pay, was a stepping stone job on my journey to living my dreams. Even though it was a great job, after a decade, the Universe started giving me signs that it was time to pack my bags and head in a new direction.

The quiet voice within me said, "It's time to move on. Don't get too comfortable. That wasn't your final resting place!"

I'm grateful that I heard the voice and that I listened. I've learned that when I don't LISTEN to my inner voice, it creates a lot of unnecessary pain and drama.

Just as I was hearing the voice telling me it was time to move on, the housing market crashed. The company I worked for filed bankruptcy and ended up firing the entire sales team.

That was my BIG sign to move on and to take my online business full-time.

ARE YOU LISTENING TO THAT QUIET VOICE?

If your life is filled with endless activities, chores, and a job that doesn't fulfill you, it's easy to miss the shhhh-ispers (as I like to call them.)

Oprah says God speaks to us in *whispers*. She also says if you don't listen to the whispers, you'll get hit with a brick upside your head, and if you don't listen when the brick comes, then the walls will come tumbling down around you, and if you still don't listen, then the house will come crashing down.

When things are off course in our lives, the Universe is always trying to get our attention with "WAKE UP CALLS" – they are literally calling to WAKE YOU UP to your SOUL! Sometimes they are drastic in the form of health issues, family issues, job loss, relationship change, etc. You can't ignore the signs because they will only get louder and louder.

Time outs are an essential part of this journey. It's your next step to creating the life of your dreams. Start planning your TIME OUTS now! The sooner you do this, the less pain you will have to endure.

LIST 3 WAYS YOU CAN CREATE TIMEOUTS IN YOUR LIFE

1. _____
2. _____
3. _____

EXAMPLES:

- Cut down or remove activities that you volunteer for that you really don't want to be doing.

- Take a vacation or mini-vacation to the beach by yourself.

- Carve out some time for solitude in your house to reflect and do your soul's work.

- Take a few hours out of your weekend to be by yourself and do nothing.

MENTAL TIME OUTS

Years ago, I was having trouble falling asleep and staying asleep. My mind was always on full speed, and I didn't know how to slow it down. Luckily, I discovered meditation and the numerous mental and physical health benefits I learned about persuaded me to give it a try. There were many studies done on the physiological benefits of meditation that I couldn't overlook; it was a great way to calm down my monkey mind.

Slowing down my overactive mind for two minutes seemed like an eternity in the beginning. I knew it wouldn't be easy, but I stuck with it and I can tell you whole-heartedly that meditation changed my life. I am a huge advocate of meditation as I truly believe it will help you take a quantum leap toward your dreams.

Now, I practice meditation at least 20 minutes a day in the morning; and sometimes in the evening. It has helped me hear my own quiet voice, and it also drowned out the voice of others.

Recently, I made a pact with God that whenever God was thinking of me, to show me a sign, which I chose to be a red cardinal.

Right after I made that pact with God, I was sitting outside in my backyard, under a shaded tree in late August writing this chapter. Just as I wrote the words, "Meditation changed my life," a beautiful red cardinal landed a few feet from my lounge chair. Actually, the red cardinal is back. I can see this beautiful creature as I am writing these words to you.

God, your Higher Power, the Universe, whatever you like to call the creative life force of everything that is, can easily be found in quiet spaces and in nature. So, if you want to connect with this Higher Power, create some space in your mind and in your life to hear the whispers. Creativity flourishes when we give it space. I believe this is where "million-dollar ideas" come from because nature abhors a vacuum.

Meditation has a way of bringing us back to the present moment. We learn through practicing meditation to pay attention on purpose and without judgment.

One of the books that helped me learn about meditation that I mentioned earlier was, *Wherever You Go, There You Are* by Jon Kabat-Zinn. Here are a few words about meditation from Jon's book:

"Meditation is simply about being yourself and knowing something about who that is. It is about coming to realize that you are on a path whether you like it or not, namely, the path that is your life. Meditation may help us see that this path we call our life has direction; that it is always unfolding, moment by moment; and that what happens now, in this moment, influences what happens next."

You are the co-Creator of your life! How powerful is that?

A Course in Miracles says: "There are no neutral thoughts – we are always creating on some level."

Do you want to be present to this creative process of your life?

Meditation is a tool that will engage you and wake you up to the authentic you and to your life's path.

One warning, though, DON'T use meditation as an escape to be fully engaged in your life or to avoid the parts of your life you'd rather not deal with.

You might also need to take an intermission from technology to create more time and space in your life.

HOW TO BREAK UP WITH YOUR PHONE

While at a book festival recently with my father, I picked up the book, *How to Break Up with Your Phone*, by Catherine Price. I actually thought I would give it to my kids, but once I started reading it, I realized I needed it more.

Because I have an online business, I felt like I was attached at the hip to my phone, computer, laptop, and iPad. I also was experiencing increased back and neck issues which was from spending way too much time at the computer and on my devices.

A FEW INTERESTING STATISTICS I LEARNED FROM THIS BOOK:

- Americans check their phones on average at least 47 times per day. For people between 18 and 24, the average is 82 (the numbers are consistently on the rise).

- On average, Americans spend more than 4 hours a day on their phones. That amounts to about 28 hours a week, 112 hours a month, or 56 full days a year.

- Nearly 80% of Americans check their phones within a half hour of waking up.

- Half of us check our phones in the middle of the night.

- We're checking our phones so much that we're giving ourselves repetitive strain injuries such as "texting thumb," "text neck," and "cell phone elbow."

- Nearly 1 out of every 10 American adults admits to checking their phone during sex.

Once I started reading this book, I realized there was an imbalance in this area of my life, and I needed to make some changes.

In 2017, a *Stress in America* report by the American Psychological Association said two-thirds of American adults agree that periodically unplugging or taking a DIGITAL DETOX would be good for their mental health.

The triggers that helped me realize I needed a DIGITAL DETOX were:

- ✓ My back completely went out on me for almost a week after being glued to the computer working on client projects.

- ✓ My body felt stiff all the time.

- ✓ I would watch webinars and read eBooks on my phone in the middle of the night, then was not able to fall asleep.

- ✓ My sleep patterns were interrupted.

- ✓ When I didn't check my phone dozens of times a day, I felt anxious like I was missing out on things (FOMO – FEAR OF MISSING OUT – is real).

- ✓ After I installed a screen-time tracker I saw that I was in fact spending four hours plus on my iPhone daily and additional hours on my desktop computer and laptop.

- ✓ My attention span was getting shorter and shorter.

✓ My memory seemed weaker.

✓ My brain felt "tired" all the time like I had brain fatigue and brain fog.

✓ I could not find the time to create content for my online business and write my own books!

I couldn't understand how I was the boss of my 6-figure business and I couldn't find the "time" to work on my own book projects.

The number one culprit I discovered was FACEBOOK!

It was easy for me to make the excuse that I was on Facebook because of my "online business," but the truth of the matter was that I was doing mindless scrolling, watching videos, watching webinars from sponsored ads, and not doing any "work".

So, I deleted the Facebook app from my iPhone.

And guess what happened?

I found 2-4 hours a day to create content (writing blog posts, online courses, and books) and it's been amazing ever since.

At first, I thought I would have FACEBOOK withdrawals, but the opposite happened – I felt FREE!

And not only did I feel FREE, I felt grateful I discovered the book *How to Break Up With Your Phone* because I didn't know just how insidious this technology problem I had was and how it was stealing away my dreams one post, one scroll, one email, one tweet, and one text at a time!

Until I became aware of the problem, I was operating in default mode which is how many of us operate especially when it comes to technology.

WHAT I LOVE ABOUT CATHERINE PRICE'S BOOK IS HOW SHE BREAKS IT DOWN INTO TWO PARTS:

1. **The Wake Up** – Educate readers about how our iPhones are designed to addict us and what they are doing to our sleep, our memories, our attention spans, and our lives.

2. **The Breakup** – How to breakup with technology (not in an all-or-nothing event but create a new healthy relationship with technology that does not steal your life away).

In her book, Catherine Price, says:

"In order to maximize the amount of time we spend on our devices, designers manipulate our brain chemistry in ways that are known to trigger addictive behaviors. Most of these techniques involve a brain chemical called dopamine. Dopamine has many roles, but for our purposes, the most important thing to know is that, by activating pleasure-related receptors in our brains, it teaches us to associate certain behaviors with rewards (think of a rat that gets a pellet every time it presses a lever). Dopamine makes us feel excited – and we like feeling excited. Any experience that triggers the release

> ### *of dopamine is therefore something that we'll want to experience again."*

So basically, we are bombarded with these online triggers (likes on our Facebook posts, shares, multiple likes on Instagram, etc.).

Unfortunately, phones and apps are deliberately designed without *"STOPPING CUES"* to alert us when we've had enough. This is why it's so easy to accidentally binge and not realize you have a problem.

> ### *Our brains just want more dopamine – again and again and again!*

So, this isn't about a lack of willpower on your part, this is about technology designers deliberately manipulating our dopamine responses to make it extremely difficult to stop using their products.

Remember, this chapter is about removing things from your life in order to create more time in your life to explore, imagine, and design your dream life.

I fully believe that technology is a double-edged sword. It has advanced society in many ways, but it's also negatively affecting the way we relate to people, interact with one another, and can cause physical problems when we binge on technology.

The truth is that it's easier to check Facebook or Instagram or write a Twitter post than it is to work on your dreams or, in my case, write a book.

WHY?

Because we all have an inner demon called "**RESISTANCE**."

Stephen Pressfield, author of *The War of Art* says this about resistance:

"There is an enemy. There is an intelligent, active, malign force working against us. Step one is to recognize this. This recognition alone is enormously powerful. It saved my life, and it will save yours."

We all have resistance when it comes to pursuing our dreams, our art, and our passions.

The more barriers we can remove like **technology addiction**, the more successful we will be.

If you feel like you are spending too much time on your devices, I suggest reading Catherine Price's book and creating a new relationship with technology that gives you the time and space you need to create your dream life.

RITUALS AND INTERMISSIONS

Carl Jung knew how to create daily rituals and take intermissions in order to do deep work.

According to journalist Mason Currey, author of *Daily Rituals*, Jung would rise at 7 a.m. and after a big breakfast, he would spend two hours of undistracted writing time in his private office. His afternoons would be filled with long walks in the countryside and meditation. In 1922, Jung built a two-story stone house retreat he called *the Tower*. Jung once said, "In my retiring room, I am by myself..." and "I keep the key with me all the time; no one else is allowed in there except with my permission. There was no electricity at *the Tower* and Jung was in bed by 10 p.m. Jung went on to say, "The feeling of repose and renewal that I had in *this tower* was intense from the start."

The tower was not an escape from work, but more of a space to advance his work. In order to do his deep thinking, he needed to be alone with his thoughts.

It might sound strange, but we live in a noisy world and we need to be alone with our thoughts in order to do our deep work.

In his bestselling book, *Deep Work*, Cal Newport defines the term deep work as:

"Professional activities performed in a state of distraction-free concentration that push your cognitive capabilities to their limit. These efforts create new value, improve your skills and are hard to replicate."

Jung built a *tower* of stone in the woods to promote deep work and the payoff was massive.

It isn't easy to prioritize our own *deep work*, but if you want to create your dream life, it's absolutely imperative to do so.

In order to get my writing done, I have to organize my life in such a way that I get lots of long, consecutive, uninterrupted time by myself.

When I was checking my emails, Facebook, Twitter, text messages, etc., I was trading my time as well as my dreams for this technology-induced dopamine fix like an addict. My time was fragmented, and as a result, so were my dreams.

I've developed a new relationship with these devices by adding some new rules.

HERE ARE SOME OF MY NEW TECHNOLOGY RULES:

- No Facebook app on my phone; I check Facebook 1-2 times per day when I'm at my desktop computer.

- No phone next to me when I'm writing content (books, blog posts, courses) as it is distracting.

- No phone in bed with me at night.

- No watching videos, webinars or reading on my phone in bed two hours prior to going to sleep.

- Unsubscribe from email lists I no longer needed so I only get emails from people I want, and that gives me more time to read and enjoy those emails.

- No phone during meals with others.

- Deleted all apps I was no longer using.

- Have only apps and tools on my phone's home page that improve my life without stealing my attention.

- Turned off all notifications.

- Leave my phone on vibrate all the time.

> *Once you balance the time you spend on technology, you will free up more time to work on creating a life you don't want to run away from.*

We all need white space to "hear the still small voice." That's why taking an intermission, creating rituals, meditating and unplugging from technology will open the communication lines from your soul to your heart and to your head.

In the next chapter, we're going to talk about "energy vampires"; those people, places and things that steal away our energy, time and attention and show up as distractions that prevent us from living our dream life.

CHAPTER 6

REMOVING ENERGY ZAPPERS

"A high-quality life has much more to do with what you REMOVE from it than what you add to it."

~Cheryl Richards, author of
Standing Up for Your Life

Energy zappers come in a variety of forms such as: unfinished projects, negative people, physical and emotional clutter, an unhealthy lifestyle, and any activities that don't move you closer to your dreams, mission, and purpose (even if you haven't figured that out yet).

To create the time and energy required to transition out of your 9 to 5, you need to identify and remove as many of the *energy zappers* in your life as possible.

Years ago, I made a list I titled **"Top 10 Things that are Draining my Energy"** and on that list was:

1. Non-profit paperwork (I had a non-profit at the time)

2. Office Clutter

3. Paper Clutter

4. House Projects

5. Dry Cleaning

6. Yellow Page Ad

7. Garage Clutter

8. Horseback Riding Lessons

9. Boyfriend issues

10. Son's bills

For a year, I worked on removing many of these top energy drainers from my life, and in 12 months, I removed 8 out of the 10. I was very proud of myself! Eventually, I removed ALL of the top energy drainers.

Many times, these *energy zappers* are deep subconscious blocks that manifest as self-sabotaging distractions that keep us from moving forward, evolving, and growing. Often, we feel like these energy zappers are beyond our control, and we are helpless victims who cannot change the situation.

One distraction I have in my life that is a repeating pattern: dysfunctional relationships with men. Jealous boyfriends, clingy boyfriends, emotionally unavailable boyfriends, partying boyfriends, narcissistic boyfriends, etc.

As I looked back on my life, I realized that I allowed these unhealthy relationships to occupy too much time in my life and more importantly, I was so distracted by trying to fix these relationships that I wasn't working on my own life and my own dreams. I used my personal energy trying to fix men instead of building and creating my own dreams! I was putting others needs ahead of myself.

In fact, one time I was a speaker at a women's conference in Florida, I had an epiphany during one of the written exercises we were doing: every time I was creating something BIG in my business and in my life, I got involved in a dysfunctional relationship with a man. It seemed like an *unintentional* distraction (like I was a victim of circumstances), but I had to face the truth that I was choosing these types of men, and I was wasting a lot of time on them. I allowed these distractions for a myriad of unconscious emotional reasons (which I have worked on in therapy), and by doing the hard inner work. As a result of doing this work, I am now living my dreams full out.

I finally recognized this pattern in my life and sought support to heal the emotional issues that caused me to be attracted to these types of men. I am happy to say, I am a **RECOVERED JERK MAGNET**! I now have strong boundaries around my time and my life. I am focused on my dreams and do not allow dysfunctional relationships and distractions to block my dreams.

I don't want you to think that this process was easy or fast; it was not. It took years to work on these underlying emotional and spiritual issues regarding relationships and my long-held patterns, but it was worth the time, money and energy I spent getting support and help in order to heal.

Recently, I spent over a year working with three different healing professionals that helped me get to another layer of my deep-seated patterns and issues. It was one of the hardest years of my life breaking these emotional patterns.

Think about things that are going on in your life right now that seem like they are beyond your control. Now, I want you to write them down. We will look at them more closely in a minute.

Let's begin with your Top 10 List of Energy Vampires

List whatever pops into your mind without thinking too hard about it. What are the top 10 energy vampires in your life right now? Don't worry about how long they will take to remove, just write down the top 10 things (top of mind) you feel are preventing you from living your dreams.

For example, the "house projects" item I had on my top 10 list took me almost two years to complete. Mainly because I procrastinated about the work that needed to be done. If I had just done the repairs as they came up, I wouldn't have had such a long list. When I made my top 10 list many years ago, I decided I needed to de-clutter every room in my house. My office alone took three months to do!

Removing energy vampires in your life is an important part of the process in creating your dream life and that's why I wanted to devote an entire chapter to it. Remember, this section is about CLEARING things out. We need to clear out the old in order to make room for the new.

We all have blind spots, and my goal is to help awaken you to the energy that is being extracted from you every day that you could be using to follow your dreams and create a life you love.

Let's take a look at each category and begin the process of identifying your biggest energy zappers so you can take *action* to remove them.

Vision without action is a daydream.
Action without vision is a nightmare.

~Japanese Proverb

UNFINISHED PROJECTS

What unfinished projects are lurking around in your home and in your life? Do you have tax returns that need to be filed from three years ago? Do you have a room that you started painting and never finished? What about that pair of slacks hanging on the treadmill in your bedroom that just needs a new button sewn on? Or the half-finished craft projects in boxes you were going to get to last Christmas?

The goal is not to get rid of your to-do list once and for all because that is an unrealistic goal. The immediate goal is to remove the projects that have been on your to-do list for too long. You know, the ones you've been procrastinating about for months, if not years!

The purpose of your to-do list is to better organize your time, so important tasks and appointments don't slip your mind. A lot of people do the easiest tasks first, crossing them off the list and then transferring the dreaded tasks from week to week and from list to list. *Sound familiar?* I know. I've done this many times myself.

If you're serious about quitting your job and following your dreams, you're going to have to free up all that psychic energy that is being drained from you by these energy zappers.

Every day, review your top 10 energy zappers that you wrote down and start removing them from your life. Simplify your life so you can focus on what's important to your heart and soul.

ACTIVITIES THAT DON'T MOVE YOU CLOSER TO YOUR MISSION

Remember the mission statement you wrote down in Chapter 3. If you didn't do the exercises, GO BACK AND DO THEM NOW. Having a mission statement will make your life easier because it will act as a guiding light to help you know when to say "*YES*" to requests and when to say "*NO*."

In 1999, shortly after I wrote my mission statement (*My mission is to inspire, motivate and educate others to believe in themselves and find their true purpose in life*), I received a call from a friend who had a "business opportunity." Because I am very curious by nature, and the fact that I am a recovering people pleaser and don't like telling people NO, I typically would spend lots of time listening to what others had to say about these "business opportunities." I can't tell you how many network marketing activities I became involved in until one day I grew tired of these companies changing the structure of their compensation plans; I finally realized I wanted to build my own business and dreams instead of someone else's.

On this particular phone call, with my mission statement hanging on the wall right in front of me in my office, I listened for a few minutes, but when this person asked me to spend more time on a conference call with her boss to give me "additional information" about the business opportunity, I kindly declined. I told her that the opportunity she mentioned was not in alignment with my mission. I also explained that I needed to stay 100% focused on my mission and goals.

I have done this repeatedly since then. As you probably know, there are a lot of great business opportunities, projects and ventures you could get involved in; but the question for you to ask yourself is: *Is this opportunity, project or venture moving me closer to my mission or not?* If the answer is NO, then only go back to the activities that will help advance you towards your mission.

Always keep in mind, however, that it is okay to explore and test things out as we discussed earlier with vocation vacations and test driving jobs to find clues that will help you create a new future. Use your mission statement as a guiding light to make decisions.

REMOVING EMOTIONAL AND PHYSICAL CLUTTER

I am by no means an expert in emotional clutter, unless you want to count the fact that I've carried my own emotional baggage around with me for years and I spent many more years in therapy unloading it.

So, how do you know if you have emotional clutter? There are clues.

First, look to your relationships.

Ask yourself, "Is there a lot of drama, hurt, pain and disappointment?"

If the answer is YES, that is **Clue #1** that you haven't fully released the past including the pain, resentments and grudges that we all hang on to. Once you release these, your life will become much calmer and more peaceful. If your relationships are not peaceful and conflict-free, then you probably have unfinished business somewhere in your past. When you clear up that unfinished business, the emotional clutter will be released and will no longer be an obstacle to creating the life of your dreams.

Emotional clutter is like a blocked artery to the heart. My advice is do the deep work (the work you don't want to do) to process it or it will kill your dreams and visions.

In order to clean up my own emotional baggage, I worked with a trained therapist, an energy healer, read self-help books and worked with a spiritual counselor who helped me find the buried emotional blocks I wasn't even conscious of. This was important work in my journey to living my dream life. I also worked with a practitioner who specialized in trauma, emotional issues and grief work.

A great book I recommend about healing and resolving past trauma is *Waking the Tiger* by Peter A. Levine

In his book, Levine lays out the steps needed to heal trauma from life's events.

He also makes an important point that trauma can come from any of the following experiences:

- Victims of physical and mental abuse

- Soldiers and war-related events

- Natural disasters such as earthquakes, tornadoes, floods and fires

- Accidents and falls

- Serious illnesses

- Sudden loss

- Surgery and other medical procedures

- Large-scale social traumas

- Mass shootings

- Difficult births

A trauma is anything that causes a frozen residue of energy in our bodies, minds and souls that has not been resolved and discharged. This residue remains trapped in the nervous system where it can wreak havoc on our bodies and spirits causing long-term alarming, debilitating symptoms such as PTSD.

So it's important to know that if you find yourself stuck and unable to move forward in your life, you may need to heal past traumas.

Clue #2 is that you have a strong emotional reaction (over-reactions) to certain situations that happen in your life.

Clue #3 is that certain situations keep repeating themselves.

Unfortunately, sweeping the emotional clutter under the rug isn't an option when you are creating your dream life because these dramas and traumas will repeatedly block you from your dreams.

Often, when we look back at our lives and create a timeline of events, we begin to see a pattern emerging.

So, what can you do about emotional clutter?

It would be nice if we could just visit the doctor, go under anesthesia, and have all our emotional baggage removed in an outpatient visit. We live in an instant gratification world but removing emotional baggage does not happen instantaneously.

HERE ARE A FEW SUGGESTIONS BASED ON MY OWN EXPERIENCES:

- Visit a therapist and start talking about it; you would be amazed at how freeing it is to simply talk about it and release your past.

- If you've done a lot of "talk" therapy, then work with an energy healer who might be able to help you remove emotional blocks in your body.

- Go to a spiritual counselor who is an expert at identifying and removing emotional blocks.

- Visit a "Re-birther" to see what pain from your past is blocking you in your present; I did this, and it helped me tremendously.

- Do forgiveness work with a trained therapist or counselor.

- Purchase a journal and write it down. Remember, what doesn't get ex-pressed becomes de-pressed. Get it all out!

- Cry all the tears you held back over the years. Holding back our emotions is not only damaging to our emotional health but it is damaging to our physical health as well. When we hold back our tears, they are stored in our bodies and fester in our bodies until we find ourselves at the doctor complaining about things like ulcers, insomnia, and high blood pressure. Rent some sad movies and give yourself permission to cry it all out.

- Face the fears that are holding you back from moving forward in your life– fear of failure, fear of success, fear of the unknown, fear of rejection, fear of change (this is a BIG ONE!), fear of being judged, fear of not feeling deserving or worthy. Fears are what keep us playing it safe – they keep us "camping out," and they keep us stuck in status quo mode. Anyone who is successful has faced their fears to achieve higher levels of success. You never know your potential unless you bite off more than you can chew. In the past, I've scheduled classes to teach before I ever put the program together because I knew it would motivate me to action and enable me to overcome my fears at the same time. I took action in spite of my fears, and you can do the same.

- Tell the truth to yourself and to others.

FINDING MY VOICE

After working with an energy therapist for several months to remove some long-standing emotional blocks in my body, I discovered that my throat chakra was completely closed off.

During one session, I sensed and actually visualized a golf ball lodged in my throat. At the time, I was in an on-again off-again eight-year relationship. One of my complaints in the relationship was my boyfriend was obsessed with golf. It wasn't the golf per se that bothered me, but rather how he avoided intimacy and emotional connection with me by using golf as an escape. The golf ball represented all the times during our relationship that I did not speak my truth.

I believed I had to hold back my voice to preserve the relationship. My fears that the relationship would end kept me silent. The more I held back my true feelings and thoughts, however, the more emotionally disconnected we became until finally a crisis occurred causing us to separate.

In her book, *Silencing the Self*, author Dana Crowley Jack discusses a condition called the divided self.

"The woman begins to experience two opposing selves; an outwardly conforming, compliant self, and an inner, secret self who is enraged and resentful. Trying to live up to external standards, a woman creates a 'dark double' – an accompanying shadow self that undermines her attempts to be a loveable woman."

Through Speaking Circles® and personal therapy work, I became more consciously aware of my own divided self. I began to notice the thoughts I had were very different, if not completely opposite, to the words I spoke.

Ironically, in my intimate relationships, I was striving for more intimacy using deception as the means to get there. As I began to wake up, I discovered that one of my unspoken needs in my relationships was "security," and in exchange for security I repressed my voice. My needs became distorted, and the price I paid was a loss of self-worth and an inability to show my true, authentic self within the relationship. The distance between who I appeared to be and who I really was grew larger every day.

As young children, one of our needs is to be accepted and loved; as a result as we get older, we sometimes had to repress our true thoughts and feelings in order to get these needs met.

For many of us, showing emotion was unacceptable. I was not allowed to show anger or hurt, and I was taught to play the nice girl role all the time regardless of how I truly felt. One of the phrases my mother often said during my childhood was *"Children should be seen and not heard."*

Repressing our truth and our voice is the birth of the divided self – the *"conforming, compliant self"* and our dark double.

If any of this sounds familiar, ask yourself *"What is the pay off?"*

Check in often throughout each day to see if your thoughts match the words you are speaking. If they don't match or are not even close, you may be operating from your divided self.

Make friends with your divided self; find out what she is trying to gain. We can speak our truth and get our needs met, but it isn't always easy. And sometimes we speak our truth and the relationship ends. If that happens, then the person you were in the relationship with wasn't comfortable with you being your true self.

Do you really want to be in a relationship where you aren't able to be the real and authentic you?

I SPOKE MY TRUTH AND THE RELATIONSHIP ENDED

I am happy to say I ended a four-year on-again, off-again relationship when I realized the more truth I spoke in this relationship, the worse things got until finally I could no longer take all the drama, stress and anxiety in my life. I had enough. I was tired, drained and I finally made a conscious choice to choose myself and my dreams over this drama filled, high-conflict relationship with an extremely narcissistic and manipulative man.

Staying emotionally balanced isn't a one and done event; it's an ongoing process we have to work on throughout our lives. Some tools that help me stay emotionally balanced and peaceful are meditation, yoga, journaling, walking, exercise, organizing my *stuff*, taking mini vacations, being near the water, getting together with my friends, seeing my children and grandchildren, and talking to a counselor or therapist if needed.

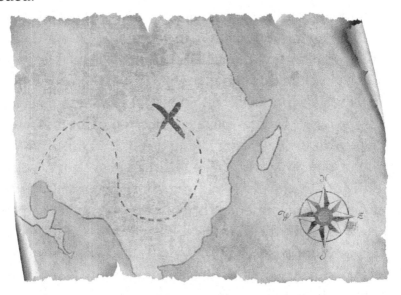

Write down some activities that keep you emotionally balanced or that appeal to you and start doing them.

PHYSICAL CLUTTER

Just as emotional clutter can block the energy required to live our dreams, so can physical clutter. It can affect us physically, mentally, emotionally and spiritually. As we begin to clear up the clutter in our homes and in our lives, we release the "stagnant" negative energy, which creates space for new energy to come into our lives.

There are so many excuses about why we don't want to get rid of our clutter; here are some common excuses not to clear out the clutter:

- **I might need this someday.**

- **It has sentimental value.**

- **I have so much, I don't know where to begin.**

- **I don't have the time, money or energy to declutter.**

These all seem like valid excuses, but the fact is your clutter is keeping you from your dreams.

You do have a choice, though. You can remove the clutter or remove the possibility of ever achieving your dreams. It's that serious. You've got to get rid of the old to make room for the new. This process involves a lot of faith and trust.

So, what exactly is clutter? According to Karen Kingston, author of *Clear Your Clutter with Feng Shui*, there are four categories:

1. **Things you do not use or love.**

2. **Things that are untidy or disorganized.**

3. **Too many things in too small of a space.**

4. **Anything unfinished.**

We addressed "Unfinished Projects," already so we have three additional areas to look at.

First, I encourage you to systematically go through each and every room in your home and begin to get rid of things you do not use or love. As Marie Kondo, author of *The Life Changing Magic of Tidying Up,* suggests "remove things that don't spark joy."

I redecorated my bedroom several years ago and it was difficult to get rid of knick-knacks and so-called "decorations" that had been there for the past 10 years or more. I didn't "love" many of these items, but they seemed like they were a part of me because they were around for so long. They almost seemed like extensions of the old me. I made the tough decision before I began the project that when I looked around my room, I only wanted to see things that I absolutely loved and that sparked JOY.

Consequently, my house is decluttered and the items in it represent the true me. I only display things in my home that bring me great joy and happiness. Photos of my children and grandchildren; angel and butterfly décor; my Buddha lady statue, candles, several pieces of custom art that I love; homemade pottery; books that are meaningful to me; and a small writing desk. I can honestly say my home is a serene and peaceful environment. A place for me to retreat to when I am feeling stressed or overwhelmed, or when I simply want to relax and feel warm and safe.

I want you to feel that way about your home when you walk through the front door and when you go into any room in your house. If you don't feel that way, then it's time to start filling up boxes for a yard sale, donation, or the trash.

Clearing up your clutter isn't always about removing things from your house. It is also about *organizing the stuff you are keeping.*

When I was in outside sales, I saw a lot of houses and sometimes there was so much clutter in these homes, there wasn't a place for me to sit down to talk with the homeowners. It takes time, money and energy to organize your stuff, but once it's done, your life will work better because you'll spend less time looking for things that are lost in piles of stuff.

I can see why Marie Kondo has sold millions of books on organizing our stuff and removing clutter because our "stuff" is literally taking over our lives.

Joshua Becker, author of *The More of Less,* says:

"When we embrace minimalism, we are immediately freed to pursue our greatest passions. And for some of us, it's been a long time since we've had access to the resources required to chase our hearts' greatest delights, however we define those delights. Living with less offers more time to spend on meaningful activities, more freedom to travel, more clarity in our spiritual pursuits, increased mental capacity to solve our most heartfelt problems, healthier finances to support causes we believe in, and greater flexibility to pursue the careers we most desire."

A minimalist lifestyle can be custom created to focus on what's important to you. It doesn't have to be extreme like selling everything you own and living in a tiny house. It's just about finding balance so you can spend less time taking care of your stuff and more time on your dreams and passions.

Put a box by the front door and every day try to find one or two things to give away and start removing the clutter, or buy Marie Kondo's book and go all in.

REMOVING NEGATIVE PEOPLE

When I began to reclaim my authentic self and speak more of my truth, my whole world began to change. It was as if I was an actress in a play and as one scene ended, a new scene began only some of the old characters were replaced with new characters.

There appeared to be a natural clearing out of relationships in my life that did not support me speaking my truth. This doesn't mean when you begin to speak your truth, you will automatically lose relationships in your life; however, chances are good that there are a few people in your life who are more comfortable with you when you don't speak your truth.

Harriet Lerner, author of *The Dance of Intimacy*, says:

"People need us to be a certain way for their own sake, and for the most complex variety of unconscious reasons. Being real means being who you are in relationships regardless of what others need, wish or expect you to be."

If you've been wearing a mask in your relationships as I was (the mask of people-pleasing and avoiding conflict), when you remove the mask, there will be an adjustment period as people are not used to you speaking up and telling your truth; some people will drift out of your life because they were more comfortable with you when you wore the mask.

Speaking your truth always involves taking a risk. I had a friend I knew from high school for over 30 years. As I took small risks in our relationship and began telling her more of my true thoughts and feelings, she became more withdrawn from the relationship. Suddenly, a huge crisis was created, and my friend dropped out of my life completely.

Intimacy in relationships means being able to share our true thoughts and feelings to another human being. My client and author of *Keep Your Sexy Sacred*, Sabrina Lawton says the word Intimacy means "In To Me SEE." I love that!

It's easy to show only our "best selves" in relationships, but we are out of balance and not operating within our authentic self if we are not also expressing our weaknesses and vulnerabilities. This is the key to emotional health and well-being.

Another aspect of speaking your truth is you may find yourself in more conflicts for a short time while others adjust to your new self – which is not really a new you at all, but simply a "truer" version of the you that you've always been.

In nature, there is a constant recycling of life and death – a natural replenishing. As you begin to find your true voice, try it on with different people in your life.

Take baby steps and remember to speak your truth while connected to your heart and with compassion. It takes courage to remain true to yourself and not everyone – even those closest to you – will always support you in reclaiming your authentic self. Let nature do her work; she will always replenish what she takes away.

Trust.

AN UNHEALTHY LIFESTYLE

Adelle Davis once said, "As I see it, every day you can do one of two things: build health or produce disease in yourself."

Which one are you up to these days?

It seems to me what she is really saying is, if you aren't taking care of yourself daily, eventually that neglect will catch up with you in the form of disease.

Unfortunately, many people don't value their health until it is taken away from them. The foundation of your happiness and your future is built on taking care of yourself NOW.

Years ago, I met a man on a sales appointment who was having all of his teeth pulled and replacing them with dentures. He was probably in his late 40's or early 50's, and I remember the comment he made to me that day, *"This is a result of 20 years of neglect."* He didn't go to the dentist because he didn't *like* the dentist; so in the end he suffered a huge loss.

One of my favorite sayings is: "If you do what is easy, life will be hard. If you do what is hard, life will be easy."

Everyone knows what is required to take care of ourselves; in fact, it's pretty simple – proper nutrition, exercise on a regular basis, low-stress, plenty of sleep, and balance.

So, if we all "know" this, why do many of us neglect these areas in our lives? The most common excuses are lack of time, discipline and/or the energy to do something about it.

There's a Spanish proverb that says:

"A man too busy to take care of his health is like a mechanic too busy to take care of his tools."

Your body is the tool you need to achieve your dreams. Your body takes you from place to place, and that requires a certain level of energy. If you aren't taking care of your body, the energy levels won't be there to sustain your dreams. This is a life and death issue; either your dreams live or they die.

Which one do you choose?

Creating the life of your dreams requires a tremendous amount of energy. Anthony Robbins says this about energy:

"The higher your energy level, the more efficient your body. The more efficient your body, the better you feel and the more you will use your talent to produce outstanding results."

I believe the type of people we choose to surround ourselves with is also important to our long-term success as well as the types of books we read. So, if you want to get healthy, start hanging out with healthy people and read books frequently about health to inspire and motivate you. Of course, hanging around healthy people and reading books about good health won't do anything for you if you don't take action and implement healthy habits.

When my energy levels get low, I know it means I've neglected my morning routine.

HERE'S WHAT MY MORNING ROUTINE LOOKS LIKE NOW (IT HAS EVOLVED OVER THE YEARS):

- **20 minutes of meditation**
- **Yoga**
- **Daily three-mile walk**
- **Lifting Weights**
- **Gym 2-3 days a week**
- **Reading a chapter or more from my spiritual books**
- **Journaling three pages every day**
- **Listing five items in my gratitude journal**
- **Drinking a Green Smoothie, Fresh Juice, Overnight Oats or an Acai' bowl**

- **A warm shower**
- **30-minutes spent in nature and in the sun**
- **Creatively expressing myself**

Matthew McConaughey, a famous actor, has a great rule: "...to break one sweat a day...whether that's going for a run, whether that's dancing, whether that's making love – just break a sweat a day."

In fact, researchers at Duke, Harvard and Stanford have shown that exercise is not only good for your body, but it is a powerful antidote for depression and anxiety. According to Duke, the researchers found that adults who worked out for 45 minutes a day (30 minutes of aerobics and 15 minutes of warm-up and cool-down) did equally as well as the group who took the prescription medication. They also did a six-month follow-up on these groups. Those who exercised fared better than those who took the medication and had a lower chance of relapse (8% vs. 38%).

The key to transforming your life
is to live an examined life.

We all have bad habits, and that's because we're often living our lives in default mode. When we want to change our life and get out of the default mode, a great way to do that is by changing our habits.

In his book, *Atomic Habits*, author James Clear shares the story of how the fate of British Cycling changed one day in 2003. At the time, professional cyclists in Great Britain had endured nearly 100 years of mediocrity until they hired Dave Brailsford as the new performance director. Since 1908, Great

Britain had only won a single gold medal at the Olympic Games and had failed in the Tour de France.

Brailsford was committed to one strategy: "**THE AGGREGATION OF MARGINAL GAINS**" which was the philosophy of searching for tiny margins of improvement in everything you do. Brailsford said,

---

"The whole principle came from the idea that if you broke down everything you could think of that goes into riding a bike, and then improve it by 1 percent, you will get a significant increase when you put them all together."

So that's what Brailsford and his team began doing – making small adjustments.

Here's some of what they did:

- Redesigned the bike seats to make them more comfortable and rubbed alcohol on the tires for a better grip.

- Asked the riders to wear electrically heated over-shorts to maintain ideal muscle temperature while riding.

- Used biofeedback sensors to monitor how each athlete responded to a particular workout.

- Tested various fabrics in a wind tunnel and had their outdoor riders switch to indoor racing suits, which proved to be lighter and more dynamic.

- Tested different types of massage gel seats to see which one led to the fastest muscle recovery.

- Hired a surgeon to teach each rider the best way to wash their hands to reduce the chances of catching a cold.

- Determined the type of pillow and mattress that resulted in the best night's sleep for each rider.

- Painted the inside of the team truck white, which helped them spot little bits of dust that would normally slip by unnoticed but could degrade the performance of the finely tuned bikes.

As these small improvements accumulated, and the results improved exponentially. Just five years after Brailsford took over, they won 60% of the gold medals available in the 2008 Olympic Games consequently dominating the road and track cycling events. Several cyclists went on to win the Tour de France; this became regarded as the most successful run in cycling history.

How does this happen?

According to James Clear, here's the answer:

"It is so easy to overestimate the importance of one defining moment and underestimate the value of making small improvements on a daily basis. Too often, we convince ourselves that massive success requires massive action.

Whether it is losing weight, building a business, writing a book, winning a championship, or achieving any other goal, we put pressure on ourselves to make some earth-shattering improvement that everyone will talk about.

Meanwhile, improving by 1 percent isn't particularly notable – sometimes it isn't even noticeable – but it can be far more meaningful, especially in the long run. The difference a tiny improvement can make over time is astounding.

Here's how the math works out: if you can get 1 percent better each day for one year, you'll end up thirty-seven times better by the time you're done.

Conversely, if you get 1 percent worse each day for one year, you'll decline nearly down to zero. What starts as a small win or minor setback accumulates into something much more."

We're not looking for perfection in any of the areas of your life; we're looking for small advancements. A 1% a day improvement will create huge changes in your life over time.

One of the best books I read about small changes many years ago was *The Slight Edge* by Jeff Olson.

Small changes = Big results

The changes in my life happened over a period of years. It's easy to look at successful people and miss the 10+ years they spent training and working on their craft.

Don't underestimate the power of small consistent actions to take your towards creating your dream life.

In the next chapter, we are going to be looking at one of the biggest obstacles to people being able to live their dreams – Money $$$$

CHAPTER 7

THE LESS YOU PAY,
THE MORE YOU CAN PLAY

Money is a double-edged sword. We need it to survive, we need it to enjoy life, we need it to help others and we need it in order to be generous. Unfortunately, we also use money in emotionally unhealthy ways when we aren't fulfilled and living our lives on purpose, which causes us to have fewer options and bigger obstacles to overcome while pursuing our dreams.

In this chapter, we will look at ways to reduce your expenses and get out of debt so you can buy back your time.

We've discussed the differences between a BONDAGE JOB and a FREEDOM JOB. The main difference is a FREEDOM JOB gives you a paycheck but doesn't consume your time, your energy, your soul or define you. A BONDAGE JOB sucks all of your energy, time and consumes your soul.

Tama Kieves, author of two brilliant books, *This Time I Dance* and *Inspired & Unstoppable*, was a Harvard Lawyer on the partnership track at a high-profile law firm in New York City who courageously quit her job and started waiting tables at the Paradise Café so she could write. Kieves would often write in cafés, walk in the park, journal, read and in many ways, peel off the dead layers around her heart and her intuition. She chose to wait tables because she wanted to work *desk-free*. According to Tama, for every notch of status she gave up, she gained a world of freedom.

IT'S TIME TO PUT YOUR LIVING EXPENSES ON A DIET

Years ago, I owned a 5,000 square foot, million-dollar home, which I absolutely loved. I bought it when my kids were teenagers, and it was a great family home. I purchased it with my then fiancé, and when we split up, all the bills for the million-dollar house fell on me.

After a while, it became a burden to take care of the 5,000 square foot house financially and physically. After five years, I sold that house and downsized to a 2,300 square foot one level rancher in my dream neighborhood overlooking the Chesapeake Bay. My space is quiet, serene, and I'm gazing out at the water as I write these words. It's the perfect place for me. I decreased my monthly expenses by over 60% so I could reduce my stress, focus my energy, spend time doing what I love, and enjoy my life.

One of the homes I lived in years ago had an in-law suite in the basement, and I was able to rent out that space for income. There's a show on HGTV about turning regular properties into income-producing properties. With the increasing popularity of services like AirBNB, you may be able to rent out some space in your home to generate cash. Or, maybe you can do a low-cost remodel and create an in-law suite or area to rent out if you own your home.

Instead of looking at cutting your living expenses as hard work, let's look at it as a fun adventure.

In his book, *The More of Less: Finding the Life You Want Under Everything You Own,* author Joshua Becker and creator of www.becomingminimalist.com says:

"Now, resisting consumerism won't give us happiness in itself. An absence is just a nothingness. What matters is what we fill the empty space with. But we have to start somewhere. Resisting consumerism can keep us from being deceived and can give us the possibility of finding real happiness, whatever that might look like for each of us."

Cutting expenses won't automatically bring happiness; it's about filling the empty space with meaning. Every day I get to do things that are meaningful to me – meditation, journaling, going on long walks in my neighborhood by the water, reading books, writing books, creating content for my online business, spending time with my kids and granddaughter as well as family and friends. When I was trapped in my corporate job, I didn't do anything meaningful to me. I was too busy with work responsibilities and by the time I got home, I was exhausted.

HERE'S A FEW STORIES FROM JOSHUA BECKER'S BOOK TO INSPIRE YOU:

1. Leo Babauta, a minimalist with six children, had recently moved from Guam to San Francisco with only the contents of one suitcase for each member of the family. Leo credits minimalism with helping him get

out of debt, lose weight, stop smoking and leave the job he couldn't stand.

2. Tammy Strobel lives with her husband and cat in a 128-square foot home in Portland. The Strobels' had racked up over $30,000 in debt and embraced minimalist living as a means of overcoming it. But they fell so in love with their new life that they continued living in a Tiny House even after they had retired their debt, becoming ambassadors for this housing option.

3. Annette Garland is an Irish freelance journalist based mainly in Southeast Asia. She spends most of her time in Malaysia, travels frequently to Australia and Indonesia goes to India when she can, visits Ireland and France once a year and has plenty of other countries on her itinerary for the future. It is minimalism, she says, that enables her to do all of this. Annette has no permanent home and no car. She's been a web-working nomad since January 2013, when she decided to leave France. She calls herself an *"anywhereist."*

Do any of these stories inspire you and make you think deeper about what you really want for yourself and your life?

Sondra and Markus Ray are authors of over 20 books, workshop leaders, and trainers who recently shared with me that they don't "own" anything. No house. No car. They do rent a lovely loft apartment in Washington, D.C. with a few belongings to make it homey, but not owning things gives them freedom to travel to exotic places like India, Bali, Australia, and so many beautiful places around the world to teach their seminars. They love their freedom and wouldn't trade it for anything.

I'm not the travelling type, so travelling around the world doesn't appeal to me. However, I don't own a home right now because I don't want all the unexpected expenses that go along with owning a home.

In fact, I recently heard about a study that said the happiest people don't own homes. I can tell you that's been true for me.

Lots of well-meaning people tell me renting a house is like throwing money down the drain and they remind me of the tax write-offs I'm not getting, but guess what? I have a rent payment I can afford, and I have no unexpected expenses. And if I decide I want to move, I can pick up and go somewhere new. I feel that I have freedom living here, and I love it. The other interesting thing about the house I'm renting is that the woman who owns it is 107 years old! I feel her spirit and her energy in this house. Lots of love and happiness. She told her family she doesn't want to sell her home because she might move back one day! I'm thankful she's allowing me to rent her home and enjoy it as my own. A house like the one I'm renting on the water in an upscale neighborhood would be close to a million dollars to own, but I get to rent it at a fraction of the cost.

Creating your dream life isn't about giving up everything. It's also not about holding onto everything and just trying to better organize it. Instead, it's about reducing your debt and possessions to a level that will set you free. Only you know what that level is.

DOWNSIZING YOUR DEBT

On average in the United States, we see over 5,000 advertisements per day telling us to buy more. We also consume twice as many material goods as we did just 50 years ago. The average home size has tripled and contains about 300,000 items. We own more televisions sets than there are people in the house. We have so much stuff that one out of ten Americans rents off-site storage.

We also have a personal debt problem and the average person has over $15,000 in credit card debt and the average mortgage balance is over $150,000.

You don't need statistics though to recognize that you have too much stuff or too much debt.

Let's look at some of the benefits we will reap by reducing expenses, debt, and possessions:

- **Less stress because you'll have less excess.**
- **More money – spending less and reducing what you pay out leaves more money to play.**
- **More time and energy – now you'll have more time to follow your passions and interests and pursue things that have meaning for you.**
- **Less distraction – our things are competing for our attention. When we remove some of those things, we can place our attention elsewhere.**
- **More freedom – physically, psychically, and financially. Stuff weighs us down and makes us feel heavy. Removing stuff makes us feel lighter.**
- **More happiness – more joy and happiness because we have more time and energy to spend on meaningful activities as we learn that things don't and never will make us happy.**

We already talked about reducing clutter and possessions (energy zappers), so now we are going to focus on reducing your living expenses.

Think about it this way – for every dollar you reduce in your living expenses, you get an increase in your freedom account.

Less bills = more thrills!

You can live on a lot less than you think.

Often, we fall into default mode which is high-consumerism mode and as a result we have a high amount of debt which limits our freedom. By shrinking your expenses, you increase your opportunities.

Maybe you still feel that cutting down your expenses and material consumption seems more like deprivation or restraint, or even scarcity, but I promise it will be financial liberty and the path to real freedom.

"When we're bored in our lives, in our job and we have cash, that's a dangerous place to be. Often times, we fill the hole in our lives with extravagances, vanity, excess and insanity that feel like wealth – but the truth is it's not wealth, it's DEBT and STRESS. This debt and stress is stealing away the time you could be living a more meaningful life with and creating work you love."

~Tama Kieves, author of *This Time I Dance*

We shop on autopilot and think we "need" what we're buying when the truth is the line between our needs and our wants has been blurred.

When we're in the wrong career, we turn reckless and distract ourselves with things we don't need. Reducing your expenses is the price to pay for your freedom and your ticket out of job hell.

It's time to get creative and play the game of reducing your expenses to get back more freedom in your life.

LOOK AT EACH CATEGORY AND TAKE AS MANY ACTIONS AS YOU CAN WITH THE GOAL TO REDUCE YOUR LIVING EXPENSES BY 25% OR MORE:

MORTGAGE:

- Refinance your mortgage for a better rate.
- Drop your private mortgage insurance (PMI).
- Sell your house and move to something more affordable.

RENT:

- Downsize; do you really need that 3,000-5,000+ square foot house? I know I didn't.
- Get a roommate or rent out part of your house.
- Negotiate with your landlord to reduce your rent or handle repairs for a reduction of rent.

UTILITIES:

- Turn your thermostat down and use space heaters or window air conditioners instead of heating and cooling the whole house.
- Sign up for the energy saving day that your local carrier usually has.
- Don't leave lights and televisions on when you aren't using them.
- Take shorter showers, and don't leave the water running.

AUTO:

- Refinance your auto loan and reduce your payment.
- Sell your car privately and buy a less expensive used car.
- Swap out your lease.
- Evaluate whether you even need a car.

CABLE AND INTERNET:

- Get rid of extras – premium channels, multiple boxes and DVRs, etc.
- Disable your cable – use Netflix or other lower cost options.

CELL PHONE:

- Sign up for automatic payments and save a percentage of the payment.
- Change or remove your insurance.
- Switch your plan or carrier and see if the new carrier will buy out your contract.

HOMEOWNERS INSURANCE:

- Shop around to at least 3-5 companies to get the best rate.
- Bundle your home and auto insurance.
- Look for discounts like having a home security system.

GROCERIES:

- Make a digital list on your phone and keep a budget so you don't overspend.
- Choose store brand items.
- Join the store's loyalty program to get discounts.

EATING OUT:

- Order a meal that you can make into two or three meals.
- Split an entrée with the person you're dining with.
- Scope out specials such as happy hour food discounts, weekly deals.
- Use a meal delivery service and save money on eating out all the time.

STUDENT LOAN DEBT:

- Sign up for an income-driven repayment plan.
- Ask for a deferment or forbearance.
- Refinance your student loans.

CREDIT CARD DEBT:

- Ask for a lower interest rate.
- Transfer your balance.
- Consolidate your credit cards.

MEMBERSHIPS AND AUTOMATIC PAYMENTS:

- Review your automatic renewals and cancel ones you are not using.
- Memberships to big box stores are great if you have a large family, but if you're not going there weekly, then cancel it.
- Cancel your gym membership if you don't use it.
- Cancel your newspaper and magazine subscriptions if you aren't using them.

JOIN A BARTER CLUB:

- Join a barter club and barter your services if you own a business.
- Eat out using barter dollars.
- Use barter dollars for anything you're paying cash for (I am in a barter club and I love it!)

You can cut your expenses by 25% if you work at it consistently. Write out all of your living expenses and your automatic payments and go through them one by one. It helps to see things visually. Also include those quarterly payments, annual payments, and one-time payments.

Remember: The less you have to pay…the more time you have to play.

Let's talk about debt now.

DEBT IS A THREAT TO YOUR DREAMS

Debt is the #1 threat to living your dreams. It hijacks your future and keeps you trapped in situations in which you might not want to be. When you have debt, you pay interest and instead of your money working for you, you are allowing someone else to use your money for their own benefit.

Dave Ramsey, who is the author of numerous books on finance and runs *Financial Peace University*, recommends the following baby steps to get control of your money:

1. **Save $1000 for your starter emergency fund.**

2. **Pay off all debt (except the house) using the debt snowball.**

3. **Save 3-6 months of expenses in a fully funded emergency fund.**

4. **Invest 15% of your household income in retirement.**

5. **Save for your children's college fund.**

6. **Pay off your home early.**

7. **Build wealth and give.**

Learn more at: https://www.daveramsey.com/dave-ramsey-7-baby-steps

THE LAST THING YOU WANT TO DO IS QUIT YOUR JOB AND BE STRESSED OUT ABOUT MONEY.

Dave Ramsey recommends having three to six months of living expenses in the bank as an emergency fund, paying off all debt, and then working on putting your money to work for you through mutual funds.

Chris Hogan, author of the book *The Everyday Millionaire*, has now helped hundreds, and maybe thousands of average everyday people become millionaires. It's never too late to start no matter what your age.

We live in a consumer-driven world that teaches us to buy things we want (not need) on credit, but when you do that, you're trading in your future for temporary enjoyment.

Chris Hogan says, *"If you live fake rich now, you'll retire real broke later."*

So, getting out of debt, having an emergency fund, and investing in your future is critical to living your dreams and having freedom.

In the next chapter, we will talk about reducing your hours at work and/or weaning yourself off your job to give you more time to explore and follow your dreams...

CHAPTER 8

WEANING YOURSELF OFF YOUR 9-5

Several years ago, I was teaching a workshop based on this book, *Quit Your Job and Follow Your Dreams,* when a middle-aged woman raised her hand and said "Michelle, I'm an attorney. I make six figures, have great benefits like health insurance, two months of paid vacations, a 401k, but what I really want to do is start an acting studio on the beach in Florida. I can't figure out how to do that? I'm not a risk taker like you."

My answer:

"Following your dreams isn't an overnight event. It is something you transition into."

Of course, it isn't easy leaving a 6-figure job, or any job that pays the bills and gives you great benefits, but if you're miserable every single day of your life, then you need to come up with an exit strategy.

In this chapter, we will talk about transitioning out of your job before making the BIG LEAP out of it permanently.

There are so many creative ways to create your dream life:

- Ann Patchett worked as a waitress at TGI Fridays and wrote in her spare time.
- Elizabeth Gilbert kept multiple side jobs in order to pursue her passion of writing books and didn't actually quit her jobs until a year after *Eat, Pray, Love* became a huge success.
- Toni Morrison would wake up at 5 a.m. to work on her novels before going off to her real-life career in the publishing world.

Many successful entrepreneurs kept their day jobs until their dream business was profitable and they could afford to quit.

Elizabeth Gilbert shares some advice about anyone who is pursuing their passions and creativity:

> *"People don't do this kind of thing because they have all kinds of extra time and energy for it; they do this kind of thing because their creativity matters to them enough that they are willing to make all kinds of SACRIFICES for it."*

Yes, your dreams require sacrifice.

This chapter is about transitioning out of your current job until you can afford to quit.

PART-TIME WORK CAN CREATE MORE SPENDABLE INCOME

Before I left the legal field completely, I went from full-time to part-time which provided the perfect transition out of the corporate world.

The process was very serendipitous; I had received a call from a head-hunter looking to place someone in a part-time position working 5:30 p.m. to 1:30 a.m. three nights per week in the word processing department of a huge law firm. Just 18 hours per week!

At first, I thought she was crazy. As a single parent with three children, I couldn't afford to only work part-time. To my surprise, when I looked at the numbers, I discovered I would have more "spendable income" working part-time than I did working full-time for 40 hours per week.

So, I took the leap and left my full-time job and worked part-time for the next five years. This schedule gave me the freedom I was craving and the time I wanted to spend with my kids, as well as the chance to explore my dreams.

To make this work, I created multiple streams of income:

- I supplemented my part-time income at the law firm selling candles for a company called Party Lite (an in-home party business).
- I took a part time nanny job that paid well.
- I rented out a portion of my house for extra income.
- I rented out my one-car garage to a man who had an antique car who needed a safe place to store it.
- I delivered pizza kits for a non-profit organization with my kids on the nights I wasn't working.

You may wonder how I had more "spendable income" working fewer hours. At the time, I was paying $1000 a month in daycare, about $150 per month to commute into D.C., as well going out to lunch almost every day, purchasing business attire, and being in a much higher tax bracket.

My full-time job paid $45,000+ a year with benefits. The new part time job paid $18,000 a year. Here are the hard numbers:

- My part-time job at the law-firm ($18,000/year)
- Rental income from my roommate ($7,200/year)*
- Income from the candle business ($5000+/year)
- Nanny money ($5,000+/year)
- Pizza Kit money ($3,000+/year)

I also reduced my expenses:

- Day care ($12,000/year);
- Commuting costs ($2,000/year);
- Business Clothing ($2,500/year);
- Lunches Out ($2,400/year);
- Lower tax bracket – priceless!

In the end, it all balanced out and I was able to make ends meet.

Remember that the sacrifice is temporary and it's a path forward to living your dreams and getting your life back.

Some people might be uncomfortable renting space in their home due to privacy issues. I did give up some privacy to be able to maintain the level of income I needed to pay the bills.

When you're serious about your dreams and your freedom, you will be resourceful and creative.

Think outside the cubicle prison you're in.

Working part-time was the perfect way for me to transition out of the legal field and it opened up so much energy, time and space in my life to explore and find more clues to my dreams.

The hardest part is letting go of the security that you have with your job. It's like taking away the safety net and that can be very scary.

"The magic begins when we courageously leave what we've known to trust and hope for something more."

~Nicole Williams, author of
Earn What You're Worth

I coached a woman many years ago who was making about $40,000 a year working for someone else. She knew that with her skills and talents, she could start her own business doing the same thing and double her income in the first year. Why didn't she do it? Job security.

She knew for while she would not have a steady paycheck, and she understood there was a lot of risk involved. That's why it's so important to budget, pay off debt, reduce living expenses, and create other sources of income to minimize the anxiety and fears you will undoubtedly have about making this transition.

FAITH ALSO HELPS WHEN MAKING THE TRANSITION.

Faith is knowing deep inside that you are being guided and ultimately being taken care of.

Don't, however, use faith as an excuse for not taking action.

You have to be an active participant and co-creator in your life. Don't complain about your life but then do nothing to change it. Many people make excuses for why they aren't living their dreams and remain stuck.

Kyle Maynard, a star high school wrestler who is also a congenital amputee (all four limbs), says, "I think excuses are a way for people to give up and get away from their dreams."

If you hear any excuses coming out of your mouth, remind yourself how important your dreams are and how committed you are to making them a reality.

You can be committed to having freedom even if you don't know exactly what that looks like; you just know it's not working with your current employer and living your life like you are now.

GOING PART-TIME WITH YOUR CURRENT COMPANY

Start looking within your company for part-time opportunities. Find out what the salary cut would be and make plans to supplement the cut in pay. Remember to consider that you will also be cutting expenses associated with the full-time job so you will be saving money.

Make it a habit to review and monitor jobs online. When the time is right, you will find that perfect part-time job to transition out of your full-time job; this is the quickest way out of the 9-5 corporate grind in my opinion. Finding ways to supplement the reduction in income is key. We will talk more about multiple streams of income in Chapter 10.

3 STEPS TO WEAN YOURSELF OFF OF YOUR FULL-TIME JOB:

1. **Reduce your expenses; live within your means**

2. **Switch from a full-time job to a part-time job**

3. **Create multiple streams of income**

Transitioning from your full-time job to a part-time job (either with the company you are with now or with a new company) will give you the time freedom to pursue your dreams while making enough money to pay your bills.

To work part time, you must take action to reduce your expenses, live within your means, and create multiple streams of income to replace some of the lost income.

WORKING PART-TIME IS LIKE HAVING ONE FOOT OUT OF THE DOOR TO YOUR OLD LIFE

Working part-time is a stepping-stone on the journey to your dreams. Don't underestimate the power of this step.

I had my "FREEDOM JOB" selling hot tubs for almost 10 years while I was building my online business. I didn't have a solid plan; I was following my heart, my curiosity and my passions. That FREEDOM JOB was a stepping stone to the life I have now.

If you have your finances in order and can pay your bills, you will be fine. I don't want you drowning in a sea of unpaid bills and having creditors chasing you down so you can "follow your dreams."

No Starving Artists here!

THINGS TO CONSIDER WHEN TAKING A PART-TIME JOB:

- Ask yourself, "How much of my day will be spent doing things I love and doing things I dislike or hate?" You want at least 75% of your time spent doing things you love and only 25% doing things you dislike or hate. If not, you're going to be very unhappy, and that unhappiness with spill over into your energy reserves and deplete the energy you need to pursue your dreams. So even if the money is tempting, don't do it!

- Are you a people person or a project person? Is the job in line with this preference? Make sure it is or you will be miserable.

- Can I pay all of my bills with the income from the part-time job? If the answer is No, figure out how you will supplement that income.

- Will I have the time to work on my dreams? Don't take a job that has so much responsibility that you can't sleep at night or concentrate on your dreams.

- Most part-time jobs do not offer health insurance, so do some research and find a policy that works for you. I have health insurance with Care First that is a few hundred per month. Is it the greatest insurance out there? No. But, I eat healthy, exercise, get plenty of sleep, have minimal stress and have fun so I rarely go to the doctor. In fact, I have the type of insurance that they only sell to "healthy people" (so I'm told).

- Determine what you will do with any retirement funds you have (i.e., roll them into another account).

- Save enough to cover at least 6-12 months expenses before you transition to a part-time job. This will reduce a lot of anxiety, fear and stress.

- Once you've found that part-time job that seems perfect for you and your circumstances, select a date and go for it!

CONGRATULATIONS! You are on your way to living life on your own terms!

"There is only one success – to be able to spend your life in your own way."

~Christopher Morley (1890-1957)
American Novelist and Poet

CONTINUE WORKING TOWARDS YOUR DREAMS WHILE YOU HAVE YOUR PART-TIME JOB

I did this for years by working different freelance jobs before I could go full-time with my online business. I always made sure that the "jobs" I took would not consume so much of my time or energy that I didn't have the time and energy for my dreams.

Some of the part-times jobs I had were a freelance newspaper reporter; I taught classes for the Community College; I coached clients part-time as an independent contractor.

HOW LONG DO YOU HAVE TO STAY IN THIS PART-TIME JOB?

It's all up to you. The quicker you get your finances under control, reduce your living expenses and debt, build a savings account that can sustain you while you are building your dream life, create multiple sources of income, then the quicker you can leave your part-time job.

All of these factors will determine how long you have to stay in your part-time job.

We all have different rhythms and different goals. Don't let others set the clock for you. You will know when it's time. If you allow yourself quiet time every day, you will begin to hear the voice inside that will guide you to the next right step. You will hear the call. Trust it! It will never lead you astray.

Marjory Zoet Bankson, author of *Call to the Soul: Six Stages of Spiritual Development*, says: "At the core, listening for the call is about restoring our relationship with self, with the world around us and with God."

She goes onto say:

"Each time that a call has run its course, leaving us empty and bereft of purpose, we can trust that something new will arrive... because we have experienced this barren desert time before...because we know we are in the space between calls, when the whisper of purpose is too soft to hear."

It's okay to be in between calls, but don't stay there too long. When we start experiencing those "barren desert" feelings, we know it's time to move on.

Think of living your dreams as a river you have to cross. To get to the other side of the river, there are stepping stones.

In this book, each chapter is a stepping stone to help you get to the other side.

The next section of the book is "Creation,"
and it is about Creating Your Dream Life!
You've done the work of gaining clarity and clearing things out. Creation is the next and final step in the process.

PART III - CREATION

"Take a small step in the direction of a dream and watch the synchronous doors flying open."

~Julia Cameron, author of *The Artists Way*

CHAPTER 9

THE PASSION TEST

"When you are clear, what you want will show up in your life, and only to the extent you are clear."

**~Janet Bray Attwood,
author of *The Passion Test***

Your passions are important because they are what light you up! When you get clear on your passions, the magic starts to happen and synchronistic events line up to make your dreams come true.

Everyone has a different perspective on what the word *passion* means to them. Some people say it is their interests and/or hobbies, others say it is their obsessions, and still others believe it is the things we are really good at.

Over the years, I've used different tools to help me clarify what is important to me and what I am passionate about.

The Passion Test

Janet Bray Attwood and Chris Attwood, co-authors of *The Passion Test: The Effortless Path to Discovering Your Destiny* say that our passions are "the most important things you can think of which would give you a life of joy, passion and fulfillment."

Janet and Chris created a tool called the Passion Test® which is a two-part test that helps people discover their purpose, destiny, and ways to create work that feels like PLAY.

It's important to clarify our passions because when you get clear on exactly what they are, you can align your goals with them and begin to create and design a life you truly love.

Passion Test - Part One

Write down your top 10 - 15 passions (the most important things you can think of which would give you a life of joy, passion and fulfillment) by filling in the blank to the following sentence:

"When my life is ideal, I am

_____."

It's important to begin each passion with a verb related to being, doing or having. Close your eyes and picture your ideal life and then write your list.

Some examples of passions are:

When my life is ideal…

- I am travelling the world first class.
- I am working with an enlightened team.
- I am making a difference in the lives of others.
- I am speaking to large groups of people.
- I am a multi-millionaire.
- I am a bestselling author.
- I am being of service to thousands of people.
- I am having fun.
- I am helping others create and live their vision.
- I am working for myself in my own business.
- I am living in a beautiful home on the water.
- I am hosting writers retreats twice a year.
- I am teaching online programs that help others.
- I am painting in my studio every day.
- I am hiking in nature 3-4 x per week.

We're not looking for details of _how_ you will make this happen, it's just about the feeling of joy and fulfillment when you are doing these things.

Okay, now it's your turn...

When my life is ideal, I am...

_____.

Write the top 10-15 things that come to your mind.

Passion Test - Part Two

Once you've written your top 10-15 passions, then you will select your top five passions by reviewing each one on the list and choosing the ones that are most important to you.

Start with #1 and #2. Which one is more important? Let's say it's #2. Then, compare #2 to #3 and choose which one of those is more important. If it's #3, then compare that one to #4. Go through the entire list until you end up with your top five choices.

Magic really does happen when we get clarity in our lives. It's easy for people to say _"I hate my job..."_ but when you ask someone specifically what else they want to do, most people don't have an answer. When you do these exercises, you will know what is important to you, and then you can start setting your goals based on your passion list.

Repeat this exercise every six months since you are constantly evolving and growing. What was important six months ago, might have been achieved or maybe it just isn't as important as it was and something new might take its place.

Once you are done, write your top five passions on notecards or post-it notes and place them in strategic locations in your home.

Here are some location suggestions:

✓ **Your bathroom mirror**
✓ **Next to your computer**
✓ **In the kitchen where you prep and cook food**
✓ **Next to the remote control where you watch TV**
✓ **In your car on the dashboard**
✓ **On the refrigerator**

Doing this will keep your top five passions in the forefront of your mind. Otherwise, in a few weeks, you might have amnesia about what you wrote down.

Why does this happen?

Because life happens. Life is always moving, and we are busy with multiple things. It's easy to write down our goals, but it's easier to forget them.

When you read through your passion list several times a day, they will be ingrained deep inside of you. So, when you are making decisions, you can now ask yourself… is this going to help move me forward in the direction of my passions? Is this in alignment with my passions?

STOP RIGHT NOW AND PLACE YOUR INDEX CARDS OR POST IT NOTES IN AT LEAST FIVE PLACES.

Serendipity happens when we get clear on what we want. You do not have to figure out the "how" on anything on your list; you never know what will show up in your life.

CREATING MARKERS AND SIGNPOSTS

Janet and Chris recommend once you have your top 5 passions, that you begin to create markers (a signpost that you are living your passion).

For example, let's say your passion is becoming a bestselling author.

Your markers would be:

✓ **I've written and published my book**
✓ **My book is on a bestsellers list**
✓ **I am earning income from my book**

So, take the time NOW to write out your markers and sign-posts of what will happen when you have achieved that passion.

After leaving the legal field, I read a transformational book by Barbara Stanny called *Secrets of Six Figure Women*. Stanny had an inspiring story, and she interviewed over 150 women to compare the characteristics of women earning six figures to those of women who were not making six figures.

This book inspired me so much because after 17 years in the legal field, the most I ever made was $50k per year. In fact, I can tell you, before reading that book, when I was in the corporate grind, I never thought about making six figures and I didn't even know it was possible.

After reading her book, I did something very important. I wrote the following sentence 100 times per day.

I AM MAKING 6 FIGURES DOING WHAT I LOVE

I knew in my career at the time, I was not going to earn six figures, but I really didn't know what I could do to make six figures. I just knew that I wanted to become a 6-figure woman.

I was passionate and obsessed about becoming a 6-figure woman. I didn't focus on the *how*, I just kept writing *"I am making 6-figures doing what I love."*

And guess what?

Within 18 months, I was making six figures working 20-25 hours a week in an outside sales job selling hot tubs! How amazing is that?

It was just like my serendipitous meeting with Billy Ray Cyrus in 1992, when I became obsessed with the thought *"I am going to meet Billy Ray Cyrus, he has something important to tell me that will change my life."*

I was obsessed with this thought and I truly *believed* it. Most of my friends and family thought I had lost my mind and was delusional about meeting Billy Ray; until of course, I met Billy Ray and he changed the entire trajectory of my life.

We all have two voices inside our heads; one that begs us to be practical and the other that wants us to step out on the ledge and be magical. Your soul chooses the magical path and that always feels scary.

When it comes to being practical vs. dreaming big, most people start with being practical and they end up limiting themselves.

Sometimes the reason we try to be "realistic" or "practical" is because we are afraid that if we dream too big, we will be disappointed and heartbroken if we don't achieve our dreams.

So, I'm going to challenge you to DREAM BIG anyway, and trust that serendipity will arrive to help you bring your dreams into fruition.

When I wanted to leave my job at the law firm, the guy I was dating (a very pragmatic and conservative guy) gave me dozens of reasons NOT to follow my dreams. He said my job at the law firm was a job that I should feel lucky and blessed to have and that so many people would love to have a job like I had.

In a way, he was putting this guilt trip on me and trying to kill my dreams. In fact, after that conversation, I started calling him a "dream killer." I could see his point of view knowing he started at the bottom of a company and worked his way to the top and was now making six figures. He just didn't understand the entrepreneurial and creative spirit that lived inside of me. The job at the law firm felt like a prison to me, and no matter how practical his advice was, I was never going to be happy in that prison. Thank God I didn't listen to him. In fact, we broke up shortly after that because I didn't feel supported or encouraged by him.

I've noticed that other men I've dated seemed jealous about my success, my freedom and my lifestyle. They tried to make me feel bad about what I was doing. I no longer date those types of men. Remember, I'm a recovered jerk magnet!

Be careful who you share your dreams with – there are a lot of *dream killers* and *poisonous playmates* out there. Being in a coaching group or mastermind with like-minded people is great support as you go towards creating and living your dreams.

Now that you have your top five passions,
in the next Chapter we are going to talk about
creating multiple streams of income...

CHAPTER 10

MULTIPLE STREAMS OF INCOME

Tom Corley, author of *Rich Habits*, studied the habits of millionaires during a five-year study of the rich and poor. Here's what he found as it pertains to most self-made millionaires and their income streams:

- **65% of self-made millionaires had three streams of income.**
- **45% of self-made millionaires had four streams of income.**
- **29% of self-made millionaires had five or more streams of income.**

Having multiple streams of income is the same idea as diversifying your investment portfolio. When one income stream suffers, the others make up for it.

In my last job in the legal field, they hired a new Human Resources Administrator to secretly *clean house*.

What I mean by *clean house* is she was specifically hired to get rid of the high-paid employees without laying them off or firing them so they would be ineligible to collect unemployment or receive severance pay. Unfortunately and unfairly, the law firm was *cleaning house* through fear, intimidation and harassment.

Within weeks, co-workers in my department who had worked there for 5-20 years all left. I recognized right away what was going on and thought to myself, *"They can get rid of me if they want to, but I'm not leaving here without some severance pay."*

The new Human Resources Administrator was a tall, heavy set, angry, intimidating, and very scary woman who made my heart pound just by walking in the room. I had many confrontations with this woman, and the harder she tried to intimidate me, the stronger and more resilient I became. I kept a detailed journal of everything that was happening. When I gathered enough evidence, I filed an in-house harassment complaint with our corporate office. Within 24 hours, the intimidation and harassment stopped, and the investigation into my complaint began.

After a month, I was called into a formal meeting where I was told it was determined that I did NOT have a valid complaint and that this woman was not, according to their investigations, guilty of harassment.

After working for attorneys for more than 17 years, one thing I knew for sure was they were scared to death of lawsuits from disgruntled employees and would do almost *anything* to avoid them.

In the meeting, I was informed that my department was being restructured and my work hours were changing. Interestingly, the days and hours they offered were ones they knew I would be unable to work because of my three young children.

When I declined the offer, they told me I was free to go look for another job and that they were giving me severance pay! It wasn't a lot of money, but at that time in my life, it was perfect because it gave me some paid time off with benefits to transition out of the legal field completely.

When one stream of income dries up, you better have other streams of income flowing in!

You never know when one source of income is going to dry up.

According to the special series on the Oprah show years ago titled "Debt Diet," 75% of Americans are living paycheck-to-paycheck. That's a tremendous amount of stress! There is another way to live…

DO WHAT SQUIRRELS DO

Every Fall, the gray squirrel spends the majority of its time gathering nuts and seeds so that it will have enough food to last throughout the winter.

Did you also know that the squirrel buries its food in hundreds of different locations?

Before the squirrel buries the nuts, he cleans each nut which leaves a unique scent so he can find the nut later in winter. If a fellow squirrel or another animal finds the stash, the squirrel will have food buried in other locations.

So, what do squirrels and nuts have to do with quitting your job and following your dreams?

Well, if you look to one job as your only source of income and something happens to that job, you are going to be seriously out of luck and highly stressed. The solution to this problem is to have multiple streams of income – in other words, have a lot of nuts buried in the ground!

The founder of Entrepreneur Magazine, Chase Revel, says that it is much easier *to earn $1,000 per month from 10 small businesses than it is to earn $10,000 per month from one big one.* I like "easier," how about you?

Since getting laid off from the law firm in 2000, I have maintained multiple streams of income in my life – usually 4-8 streams. Here are some of the streams I've had over the past 15 years:

- **Royalties From My Books**
- **Income From My Bestselling Author Programs**
- **Public Speaking Engagements**
- **Coaching Income**
- **Sales From Digital Courses and Information Products**
- **Website Design Services**
- **Copywriting Services**
- **Income From Events And Retreats**

Some people say that their energy feels scattered when they have too many projects going on at once. I somewhat agree with that. Most projects require more energy in the beginning when you are getting everything set up; once the project gets going and you have systems and automation in place, then you should be able to start working on creating another stream of income (project); especially if it's passive like selling a digital online course.

Of course, this isn't always the case. Some projects require energy from beginning to end, but I believe the bulk of that energy is used when you are getting the project off the ground.

EMBRACE WHAT YOU LOVE

Others may criticize or make fun at things that interest you. That's the beauty of being human—we are all unique, and we must respect each other's differences enough to let others be who they are. We must also give ourselves permission to love what we love. Some of the things I love are decorating, cooking and baking, feng shui, baking, writing, arts and crafts, and bike riding.

- **What are five talents/interests that you LOVE?**

- **What are five services that you could provide to others using these talents/interests?**

*Remember, people have to want these services. Just because we love something, doesn't always mean there is a market for it, but it's worth exploring.

START A BUSINESS FOR UNDER $100

There's a great book by Chris Guillebeau, *The $100 Startup: Reinvent The Way You Make a Living, Do What You Love, and Create a New Future*. The essence of Chris's book is the $100 Start-Up Model – profitable businesses typically run by one person with little start-up capital.

You need skills to pay the bills, and many people already have skills for which others are willing to pay.

Go to www.fiverr.com and you'll be inspired when you see how people are using their skills to get paid – skills like graphic design, editing, copywriting, cover design, voiceovers, logo design, branding, legal help, videography and so much more.

I started my business www.bestsellingauthorprogram.com in 2013 with my first client, and within two years, I was making six figures from that program. I had the skills people wanted: writing, publishing, formatting, technology skills, and launching books to multiple #1 bestsellers lists on Amazon. I've also launched books to the Wall Street Journal and USA Today bestsellers lists!

SOMETIMES YOU CAN'T FIND THE PERFECT JOB IN THE MARKETPLACE, SO YOU HAVE TO CREATE IT YOURSELF.

There's a reason why so many freelance sites like fiverr.com, upwork.com, readsy.com and others exist. Before the internet, the employment pool was more localized and people were considered for positions geographically. Now the employment pool is global. I've had assistants from other countries which is amazing.

If you have a marketable skill, there are people ready to hire you. Maybe you're an expert at Excel spreadsheets; if you are, there are people like me who would love to hire you to create custom spreadsheets for their business.

THE FASTEST WAY TO MAKE MONEY.

The fastest way I've found to make money is to offer a **Done-For-You Service**. I've learned that if you offer to give a man a fish or to teach him how to fish, the majority of time he will want you to give him the fish.

THE FOUR ARCHETYPES OF CREATING INCOME

Cathy Heller, author of *Don't Keep Your Day Job* talked about these 4 archetypes in a recent podcast I was listening to and I immediately connected with them, so I wanted to share those with you here since we are talking about how to create multiple streams of income.

1. **Creator** – You are the creator and maker of what you sell. It can be a physical product or a service, but you make it and you sell it.

2. **Teacher** – Once you've mastered something and you begin to teach it you can 10x your income. Cathy Heller took her success as a musician and started teaching her strategies to aspiring musicians and was able to 10x the amount of money she was making as a "Creator". I've found the same thing to be true in my business. Once I've mastered something, I make more money teaching it. So teaching is a great way to earn bigger money.

3. **Curator** – This is where your pull together people, events or projects. For example, I have an independent publishing company and I publish books for clients, so I am a curator. Take your passion and figure out a way to be a curator of it.

4. **Investigator** – You love your topic so much you get paid to be an investigator of it. You might start a podcast, write a blog or a book about it. Someone who

comes to mind as an Investigator archetype is Vani Hari, creator of the popular blog, www.foodbabe.com and author of *Feeding You Lies: How to Unravel the Food Industry's Playbook and Reclaim Your Health.* She is an investigator who gets paid to do research! How can you be an investigator?

HAVING ONE STREAM OF INCOME IS RISKY

It's important that you do NOT put all your nuts in one basket. If one source of income doesn't work out, it's important to have other sources coming in. I know I sound like a broken record, but it's that important. Remember, the average millionaire has 3-5 streams of income!

For so many years I lived paycheck-to-paycheck, so I know first-hand what it's like to live with exorbitant amounts of fear, stress and insecurity. It's no fun. I don't want you to have a false sense of security when it comes to your job because that false sense of security can lead you right to the poor house.

When I was in my 20s, I worked for a solo practitioner, a personal injury attorney who absolutely adored me. I loved working for him; he was quirky, funny, crazy in a good way and had a big heart. I wore many hats in that small office which caused me to mistakenly believe that the office could not function without me.

I thought I was irreplaceable—I was wrong!

I was by no means the perfect employee. I had my faults, and one time while my boss was out of town, I decided to go pick up a mattress for one of my kids on my lunch hour. I told the receptionist to cover for me in case the boss called, and she agreed. My mattress errand took much longer than I anticipated; hours later, when I finally returned to the office (in the days before cell phones), I learned that my boss was calling every thirty minutes to talk to me. I was shocked when I got back to the office and was fired on the spot!

That experience taught me many valuable lessons:

- **Everyone can be replaced.**
- **There is no such thing as job security.**
- **Have money in the bank for a rainy day because the storm is on the way.**
- **Life is less stressful when you have multiple streams of income.**

Look at Richard Branson, a British adventurer, who is a master at creating multiple streams of income.

At age 17, Branson started a Student Advisory Center, which was designed to help young people. At age 20, he founded a record mail-order company known as "Virgin" and then opened a record shop in London. He later founded a recording studio known as "Virgin Records." (He later sold Virgin Music Group, for $1 billion). Years later, Branson founded "Virgin Atlantic Airways" which is now the second largest British international airline. Branson had a television reality show and has broken several world records. The man is an amazing creator of combining his passions with providing high quality services to others.

Zig Ziglar once said, "You can have everything you want if you help enough other people get what they want."

Branson not only has fun doing so...he makes lots of money!

Phil Laut, author of *Money is my Friend* makes a very good suggestion about how long you should try out a new idea:

Now that you have an idea of what you can do to make your favorite money-making idea a financial success, ask yourself whether you are willing to stick with it, no matter what it takes, until you receive your first $100 from it. After receiving your first $100, you can decide whether you want to continue or not.

Good luck happens when you're in action.

PICK YOUR FAVORITE PROFIT PATH

My motto is: "Work less, make more."

What I've found so fascinating about running an online business is how you can make money while you sleep, and if you're sick or take a day off, it doesn't matter – you can still make money!

Some ways to make money online:

- **Affiliate Marketing (selling other people's products)**
- **Selling crafts and homemade items on sites like Etsy**
- **Selling Information Products like an Online Course**
- **Publishing Books on Amazon**
- **Coaching**
- **Consulting**

- **Training**
- **VIP Days**
- **Done-For-You Services**
- **And MORE!**

No matter how old you are, where you grew up, what kind of job you have, or what your hobbies are, you are an expert in something. Maybe you breed toy poodles or run profitable day care centers or create beautiful art or race cars. If you collected the information in your area of expertise and packaged it into an e-book or as an online course or in a coaching program, then you could begin making money with your knowledge!

Many of my clients who I've helped publish and launch their books to the #1 bestsellers list are now making thousands of dollars from their books in a variety of ways.

Their book is just the gateway to their other products and services.

Remember, you don't have to know everything there is to know about a subject, but if you know more than the average person, then you're probably an expert.

MAKING MONEY BY ACCIDENT

I want to share with you a funny story about a guy named Tom Antion who I met years ago at the National Speakers Association (NSA). Tom sold a variety of information products and taught classes about making money on the internet.

Tom taught people that they could either develop a product and then find the market for the product OR look for an already existing market and then create a product around the market.

One day, Tom stumbled upon an already existing market.

Doing some research on keywords, Tom discovered that there were over 13,000 searches per month for the keywords *"how to write a eulogy"* and over 11,000 searches for the keywords *"how to write a wedding toast."* Now Tom doesn't know anything about either of those topics, but what Tom does know is how to create information products and make money on the internet from them.

Once Tom saw that there was an already existing market for information products on eulogies and wedding toasts, Tom went to a popular site called "Elance" (now up-work.com) to find and hire a freelance writer to write two e-books: one on eulogies and one about weddings toasts. He paid the freelance writer less than $400 for each job. He then put up a simple template website for less than $50 and he began selling his e-books for $17.00.

That may not sound like a huge amount of money, but the market was already there. He took some simple, inexpensive steps and created a unique product.

Guess how much each site generates?

His eulogy site generates about $35,000 a year and his wedding toast site generates about $40,000 a year. Not bad for doing the work once and letting the money roll in month after month, year after year.

Could an extra $75k a year help you quit your job?

BUYER BEWARE

A lot of programs show you how to make money online. Some of them are legitimate, and some of them are scams. You must do your *due diligence* when it comes to "making money online" programs. Buyer Beware.

I believe the reasons most people are not successful when they attempt to start an online business are:

✓ They are not at the right stage in their online business and it does not match the program they are purchasing.
✓ The person's skillset does not match what is required for that type of business.
✓ The lifestyle the person wants does not match the type of business they are attempting to start.

Don't sign up for a $10k coaching program from a guy that says he's making $1 million dollars a month if you've never even made $1 online. There is a huge gap between where you are and where the teacher is. You most likely wouldn't even understand the industry lingo used and the learning curve would be too great for you to overcome. You would be setting yourself up for failure.

It would be better to find someone who is doing what you want to do and who is just a little further along than you are and learn from that person.

We will talk about investing in yourself shortly; it's important to do, but you have to invest in the right things.

5 STAGES OF AN ONLINE BUSINESS

- **Stage 1 - $0 to $20k – Baby**. Involves learning new skills, understanding the platform, building a website, email list, and developing and testing a service, product, or program to sell.

- **Stage 2 - $20-50k – Toddler**. You've learned the environment, the skills needed, the industry lingo, and you've laid a foundation, and this is where you get more clarity on what you want to do with your business.

- **Stage 3 - $50-$100k** – Adolescent. You've grown up quite a bit. You are committed and you know what it takes to run an online business. You know your strengths and your weaknesses. At this point, you may get some support for your business – a virtual assistant, a tech person, a copywriter, a funnel specialist, an operations manager, etc.

- **Stage 4 - $100k to $1m** – Adult with Authority. You've proven yourself online because you learned how to make six figures! Now you can decide if you want to stay at this level and run a small boutique online business or grow your business. You have increased the value you offer in the marketplace. You are investing in marketing and have a small team.

- **Stage 5 - $1m and up** – Mature Adult. You have a great team that runs your business with systems, automation and accountability. You are charging a high-ticket premium and may have multiple programs.

Do you see how if you hire a mature adult to coach and mentor you when you are at the baby stage, the material and teachings will be far too advanced for where you are at? There are things you need to learn at every stage of starting and growing an online business.

Remember the movie *The Karate Kid*? If not, it's worth watching. In the movie, Daniel, the main character, leaves his hometown and moves to Southern California with his mom but quickly finds himself the target of a group of bullies who study karate at the Cobra Kai dojo. Luckily, Daniel befriends Mr. Miyagi, an unassuming repairman who just happens to be a martial arts master himself. Miyagi takes Daniel under his wing, and trains him using unconventional methods which become the foundation for preparing him to compete against the brutal Cobra Kai.

In business, you need to build a strong foundation to build your business upon. There is a lot of training that has to happen and that takes time.

So, if you are at stage 1 or 2, then you should hire someone who is at stage 3 or 4. If you're at stage 4, then you can hire someone who is at stage 5.

Now that you understand the stages of an online business, let's talk about some of the ways you can make money online.

Three Popular Ways to Make Money Online

Selling An Online Course.

Selling an online course is one of the most popular ways to make money online, but it is not as easy as it used to be or that experts make it out to be. I started my online business in 2005 because I was teaching live workshops and it was difficult to get people to come out of their homes and to attend. I decided to put up a website and teach virtually, before it was as popular as it is now. Currently, it's a very crowded marketplace. It's not just about developing an online curriculum; you need to have an email list and a social media following and run paid ads to drive traffic to an automated webinar to sell your course. Everyone is running Facebook ads, and it's very expensive and has a steep learning curve. If you have a large social media following and an email list already, and you can tap into that, then this could be a good business model for you. For beginners with no platform, no list, no social media and no online experience it will be hard. Which leads to the next business model...

Offering an In-Demand Service

Offering an in-demand service will be the fastest and simplest way for you to make money online. It's actually the reason I have a 6-figure business with my Amazon Bestselling Author program. My main program is a **Done-For-You Service**. I went from making $3-$5k a month coaching and selling online courses to $25-$50k+ per month offering a premium service that high-level entrepreneurs, coaches, speakers, executives, and trainers want.

If you have a skillset like copywriting, graphic design, administrative skills, editing, or sales, you will be able to quickly start offering your services to already established and successful business owners like myself. I've grown a team slowly. Right now, in my business I have a Virtual Assistant who does administrative work, organization tasks, some graphics work and sets up book launches for me. I also have a Publishing Assistant who edits, formats and publishes books for me. I just added a Project Manager to organize my business and a Tech person to take care of the websites for myself and some of my clients. So, think about what skill you have that could add value to an already existing online business owner.

Coaching Is Very Lucrative

I attribute my successful 6-figure online business to the coach I hired in September 2014, Jason Nyback. Coaches are amazing! If you want to be a coach, you don't necessarily have to be certified, although that can help, but you should have a very specific niche. Don't try to be a general "Life Coach" because Life Coach Schools are certifying thousands of people and it's a crowded marketplace.

If you have knowledge or expertise in a specific area, then you can coach others who need help in that area. Let me give you some examples of niche coaches I found at the Life Coach school run by Brooke Castillo:

- **Binge Eating Coach**
- **Real Estate Coach**
- **Weight Loss Coach**
- **Autoimmune Coach**
- **Feminist Confidence Coach**
- **Money Coach**
- **Mindfulness Coach**
- **Menopause Coach**
- **Running Coach**
- **The Deep Dive Coach (one of my clients)**
- **Female Entrepreneur Coach**
- **Non-Profit Career Coach**
- **Adoption Coach**
- **Introvert Coach**
- **Stop Over-Drinking Coach**

The benefit of being associated with a coaching school and certification program is that you can use their structures, systems and support in your own business. Also, they may refer clients to you.

Those are my top three suggestions for starting and running an online business. Just know there are many other business models for you to consider.

Other Ways to Make Money Online

Affiliate Marketing

You can make money selling other people's products. This requires you to build an email list to market to, develop a relationship with your list, and find quality programs with good affiliate commissions to offer to your list.

Membership Sites

These always sound fantastic in theory – get 1000 people to pay you $50 a month and you have a $50k per month business. It's not as easy as it sounds. You have to constantly create new content and build a large following. I've done it, and I don't care for this business model.

Live Retreats

These sound great as well, but they are challenging to organize and get people to commit to attending. Consider offering the material virtually (a DIY – do it yourself), then in group coaching (DWY – done with you) and then a live retreat for people who want the in-person training and community.

VIP Days

These can be very lucrative if you have an area of expertise where you can devote a half or full day to clients and charge a premium. I work with a PR expert, Christina Daves, who does high-ticket VIP days.

Mastermind Groups

These are like group think tanks. Everyone comes with one opportunity and one obstacle and then the group strategizes together.

Certification

If you have a successful business model, you can certify people in the process or methodology. Life Coach Schools provides a certification for those who go through their program. Many of the founders were successful life coaches and then began certifying others in their methodology. Another example is Mike Michalowicz, author of *Profit First: Transform Your Business from a Cash-Eating Monster to a Money-Making Machine*. At the end of his book, Michalowicz asks if you want to be a certified *Profit First* Coach. I believe he charges $10k for the certification program. He's certified over 150 people, so he's made $1 million+ certifying others. It's a brilliant strategy, but you must already have a successful business model for this to work.

Many entrepreneurs want to start an online business, but there is a huge learning curve and a lot of predators that promise to help you go from $0 to $100k in 30 days or $0 to $1 million waiting to take your money! Run for your life from these types of offers.

Now that we've talked about profitable online businesses you can start, let's talk about why it's important to invest in yourself.

INVESTING IN YOURSELF AND YOUR DREAMS

In my early 20's, I went on a shopping spree with my best friend Kathy at Macy's one summer afternoon. At that time, we both had bad marriages, we were living paycheck-to-paycheck, and we had a lot of debt. We both had three children and were struggling to make ends meet; shopping was the way we made ourselves feel better. That day, we each found something we absolutely loved and just had to have. Kathy purchased a $250 Gucci watch (this was in the 90's, so that would be equivalent to spending about $1500 these days) and I purchased a $250 purse that was made from snake, lizard and alligator skin. I felt good about the purchase that day, but when the credit card bill came in, I was no longer feeling good.

Debt for luxury items is not a smart investment decision.

It is important to clarify the difference between investing in ourselves wisely and using debt for material things we probably don't need and luxury items.

When investing in ourselves, the implication is we are committing our money, time, and energy to reap a future benefit. Debt is a future obligation, not a future benefit.

The distinction here is there is *good* debt and there is *bad* debt.

Investing in yourself that has a future benefit is good debt.

Spending money on credit for luxury items or material things that is not consistent with your long-term goals and values is bad debt.

While creating your dream life, you are inevitably going to incur some debt along the way. Unless you have an endless supply of money, you are going to come upon situations where there will be a choice to spend money wisely or to walk away.

SMART CHOICES WILL TAKE YOU WHERE YOU WANT TO GO

Get in the habit of making *conscious* choices when it comes to your money. Take the time to step back and think about the consequences *before* you make the choice.

Nicole Williams, co-author of the book, *Earn What You're Worth* says:

"Hating a job that pays well is NEVER a good investment strategy. Not only have I lived this monumental mistake myself, I've seen many of my friends and coworkers struggle in the same trap. I've come to learn that those who hate their well-paying jobs spend a phenomenal amount of money compensating. Food, clothes, vacations – all absolute necessities for someone who hates what they do for a living. I swear, those who hate their jobs actually take home less money."

Having a well-paying job that you hate is a real dilemma. You feel unfulfilled, but you have lots of cash and credit, so to fill the void of being in an unfulfilling job, you spend, spend, spend and the reason you spend, spend, spend is because you hate your job. We can get into an unhealthy pattern of shopping and creating bad debt that keeps us imprisoned in our unfulfilling jobs. We can't leave our job because of our lifestyle, bills and debt.

Spending money on dining out, designer clothes, vacations, upgrades or improvements on your home, new cars, hobbies, is bad debt if you are not living your dreams because it is not advancing you towards your dreams. **Bad debt fills the void that living** *without* **purpose, passion and satisfaction creates.** Unconscious spending must become a thing of the past or you will continue to delay or never realize your dreams.

Here are four true stories (the names have been changed) and I want you to decide if the person in each story is creating bad debt or good debt (an investment in the future):

Case Study 1

Liz had been out of the corporate world for years and was working as a massage therapist out of her home. She recently paid off a large debt, and she was making just enough money to break even. A course related to her field of study was coming up and she really wanted to take the class. She did not have the money to pay for it in full, however, she could put it on her credit card and pay it off in the next few months. Liz decided this was a great opportunity to learn a new skill and make herself more marketable, so she charged the full amount of the tuition on her credit card – knowing that she would be able to pay it off within the next few months.

Case Study 2

Denise has been employed with the State Government for more than 10 years. Denise liked her job for years, but now she feels burnt out. She is a single parent raising three children with a little help from her ex-husband. He pays the court-ordered child support but not a dime above that for extraordinary expenses. Denise earns what the average American earns, but with three children, her expenses exceed her income. She purchased a house about four years ago, which has increased in value considerably. She constantly cashes in her equity to pay off the credit cards that help her get by. The credit cards were not used solely for necessities like food and household items, but also for expensive jewelry, clothes, vacations, fancy meals out, Christmas presents and household extras. Recently, the jewelry store which she frequents, was having a special show with rare gems. Denise decided she deserved to have nice things and purchased earrings and a necklace for two thousand dollars. She put it on a credit card and will pay for it later.

Case Study 3

Ann left the corporate field over six years ago and has doubled her income in recent years. She has no credit card debt and has a home equity loan that she has used for large purchase items such as vehicles for her teenage children (which they make monthly payments for). Ann lives within her means. Ann uses her American Express card to purchase clothing, jewelry, furniture and some luxury items knowing that she can pay it off in full the next month. It has been years since she has had any credit card debt. Ann works from home; one of the problems she has is she gets distracted from her work with household chores – she loves a clean house! Ann decided to hire a cleaning company so she could focus more on her work instead of the chores. Ann gets lots more work done these days because she knows that every two weeks, the cleaning people will be there to get her house back in order.

Case Study 4

Nicole was in a dull marriage that lacked passion. Nicole had been a stay-at-home mom for several years. Her husband paid all the household expenses so any money she earned was for extra expenses like clothes, dining out, trips, etc. Nicole has a few different side businesses but doesn't focus her energy on any one of them, so she makes a little money here and there, but nothing substantial. Recently, Nicole went on a trip and brought her money to gamble with. The money went pretty quickly with nothing to show for it.

What do you think about Case Study number 1?

It's Good debt – an investment in the future. That's right! Although Liz was just getting by, she lived above her means. She paid all her bills in a timely manner and was trying to improve her business by learning a new skill. Even though she charged the course on a credit card, she was investing in herself and her future. Over time, she was able to pay off the bill without going under.

What about Case Study number 2?

This one is Bad Debt! Denise is unhappy and that unhappiness causes her to shop excessively and purchase things she could do without. It's not that she needs to deprive herself, but she could use that money to invest in another business, a savings account, stocks and bonds, etc. to create more money. Instead, she gets caught up in materialism and the status quo and thinks jewelry and "material things" will make her happy, but they never do. They are a quick fix, but not a lasting fix, which is why Denise has to constantly go out and buy more "stuff." The void of unfulfillment never gets filled with material things.

Case Study Number 3 is actually a story about me.

This is Good Debt! I am the fictitious "Ann" and many years ago I reluctantly hired cleaning people. I knew it was an issue because I am a neat freak and it was hard for me to concentrate on my business when I knew the house was messy. A good cleaning company is worth it to me because now I have peace of mind, I feel good about it, and I have the money to pay cash for it. It's an investment in the future because it allows me to focus more on my writing and work projects instead of household chores.

Case Study Number 4 - Nicole.

Bad debt for sure! It wasn't that Nicole was spending her bill money on gambling, it's just that Nicole was throwing away money she earned into slot machines. Nicole could have invested that money in one of her businesses, a savings account, stocks and bonds, etc. Consequently, Nicole felt bad for losing money gambling.

FEELINGS AROUND MONEY

Start paying attention to how you *feel* when you spend money. Do you feel good or bad? Do you feel hopeful or hopeless? Do you feel guilty or guilt-free? Do you feel more energized or less energized? Do you feel worried or at peace? Do you feel like your decision was right or wrong?

If you can afford it, you have excess money, and are not in debt, I am all for buying and having nice things. I love luxury cars, quality jewelry, nice vacations, a beautiful home and furnishings, designer clothes, etc. In my opinion, there is absolutely nothing wrong with having or wanting "nice things." The question is first and foremost whether you can afford it, and if not, how you feel when you spend money on these things you know you don't have the money to pay cash for.

DEBT IS A HUGE DRAINER OF OUR ENERGY. IF YOU'RE TIRED ALL THE TIME, YOU PROBABLY HAVE A LOT OF DEBT

The bad feelings we get when we spend money on things we really can't afford are red flags shouting to us. **STOP. DON'T DO IT!**

What feeling are you trying to numb when you are shopping beyond your means? Many times when we examine the feeling we're running from, we often find:

- ✓ **Boredom**
- ✓ **Low self-esteem**
- ✓ **Emotional wounds that haven't been processed**
- ✓ **Repressed anger**
- ✓ **Fear**
- ✓ **Pain**

START INVESTING IN YOUR FUTURE

It's funny how we are quick to buy a designer purse or jeans but not so quick to buy a thousand business cards or hire a web designer to create a website for us.

A great way to boost your self-esteem is to stop making choices that make you feel bad and start making choices that make you feel good. I am not saying you should go into a huge amount of debt to start your own business – take small steps -- business cards, an affordable website and logo, etc.

Take actions that tell yourself: "I am important," "I matter," "My future matters." **Invest in yourself and your future**. The by-product is that you will increase your self-esteem and be in a better financial position down the road.

When I made the decision to hire a cleaning company, I said to my best friend, *"I would rather figure out how to make more money to pay for the cleaning company than to NOT have a cleaning company."* Over the years, I have developed a deep trust in myself and:

- **My ability to create and make more money.**
- **My resiliency.**
- **My resourcefulness.**

Now I have a deep trust and knowing that whatever I want or need, I also have the ability to create the money to pay for it. I don't worry about where the money will come from or even *how* it will come. I trust in myself and in the Universe to guide me. I listen to my inner voice and make decisions from that place.

Prince Charming Syndrome

A poor investment strategy many women suffer from is the "Prince Charming Syndrome."

Do you suffer from the Prince Charming Syndrome?

The Prince Charming Syndrome is a deep-seated belief and expectation that another person is going to come rescue you – save you, pay your monthly expenses, lavish you with gifts, and keep you in the lifestyle you desire to be in.

Where did this belief come from, and why do so many women have it?

Many women are taught by their parents and caregivers to look for a man to take care of them, or they watched their own mothers or female caregivers being taken care of by a man, so they learned by example. If you think about it, women have only been allowed to have money and earn money in the last 80+ years that. Prior to that, the man was the sole provider and controlled all the money while the woman traditionally stayed home and took care of the house and the children. So, on some level, we are still operating from this old paradigm even though many things have shifted and changed.

Think about these statistics found in the book *Money, a Memoir: Women Emotions and Cash*, by Liz Perle, who says,

---

"In the 1950's the number of women who out-earned their husbands was so small that the information wasn't even systematically gathered. But fifty years later, almost one in three women do and our numbers rise every year. We control $4 trillion in yearly consumer spending. We make 62 percent of all car purchases. We take 50 percent of all business trips. We control more than 50 percent of all personal wealth in this country. And we do this while shouldering the majority of family responsibilities. We've gotten caught in a time warp where our economic realities have changed faster than our expectations and identities."

What a great point Liz Perle makes – women are in a time warp.

Women are out in the world creating wealth and many times making more money than the men in their lives, but a part of us wants and expects a man to take care of us.

Sometimes we are conscious about wanting Prince Charming to come rescue us, but many times we are unconscious to it. Personally, I have been conflicted with this idea for years.

Although I have been very independent since my teenage years, there has always been a hidden part of me that fantasized about a man coming to rescue me so I could "take a break" and let someone else worry about the bills and the future for a change.

Guess what?

Prince Charming never came for me, and he's probably not coming for you either. It's a fantasy, and the quicker you can acknowledge that and move on, the quicker you can take full ownership and responsibility for your finances, your life and your future. Believe me, I understand it's hard to let go of the fantasy; in some ways, it's like giving up on a dream. However, this particular dream has no basis in reality and is simply an illusion.

Here are some great reasons why waiting for Prince Charming is a bad investment:

- **Waiting for Prince Charming is a crutch and an excuse for not taking control of your financial destiny.**
- **It puts you in a subordinate position as well as a dependent position similar to a parent-child relationship. Do you really want to be the child?**
- **Your self-esteem does not have a chance to grow because you do not have positive experiences handling money and lack the ability to take care of yourself.**

We all have a relationship with money whether we know it or not. By ignoring money issues and waiting for Prince Charming to ride up on his white horse and rescue you, you are ignoring your relationship with money. When we ignore any type of relationship, it usually falls apart.

Waiting for Prince Charming to arrive keeps you stagnant; never moving forward. If you're not evolving, you're stuck in the mud. Do you want to be stuck in the mud?

I think that's more than enough reasons for you to let go, once and for all, of the Prince CHARMING fantasy – what do you think?

In addition to the reasons listed above, I have a couple more thoughts on the subject.

Many of the women I know who said they found their "Prince Charming" tell horror stories later about their "**Prince HARMING**"... men who weren't nearly as wealthy as they led the woman to believe; men who came on hot and heavy in the beginning and then turned out to be abusive; and men who stole a woman's heart and her bank account.

My advice (WARNING) to you: If Prince Charming shows up on your doorstep, on your porch, or anywhere on your property, do an in-depth background and credit check on him. Not to be cliché, but if something sounds too good to be true, it's because it is.

Besides, what do we really know about this Prince Charming character anyway?

If we do our due diligence and don't take a stranger's word for it, we often discover Prince Charming didn't own the kingdom outright – he had several mortgages on the property. Oh, and the white horse he rode in on was a rent-a-horse that he picked up on the way to rescuing you and had to be returned by midnight; and the diamonds he brought you turns out they were really cubic zirconias!

In summary, stop investing your time and energy in the illusion that Prince Charming is coming to rescue you – he's not! It's a bad investment of your time and energy.

Instead, take that same time and energy and begin investing in yourself, your dreams, your passions and your life.

Why? Because you matter; because it's time you started believing in yourself. When we know we matter, our choices and actions reflect that belief and we spend our time, energy and money investing in ourselves!

NON-FINANCIAL INVESTING

It is important to invest in yourself financially, but not to the exclusion of other areas in your life – mentally, spiritually, physically and emotionally. We must take care of our "whole" selves because if we focus too much in one area and neglect the others, we will suffer.

I know many people who are so obsessed with making money to the exclusion of their physical health. They are severely overweight with many medical problems like high blood pressure, diabetes, high cholesterol, digestive issues, etc. You can make all the money in the world, but if you don't have your health, you have nothing!

We are spiritual beings as well. At the end of our lives, we may have accumulated treasures on earth, but none in heaven. Additionally, if we neglect our mind and our emotions, we won't experience balance and peace of mind.

Take care of your *whole* self. Invest in your whole self. I like what singer Jon Bon Jovi says about his life, "The harder I worked, the luckier I got."

The harder you work at taking the time and energy to invest in yourself and your life, the luckier you will be in life. There is no such thing as pure luck. People that appear lucky have, in reality, worked very hard to get to that place. Hard is a relative word. I work shorter hours than most, and by choice, I have created a life with a great deal of down time.

Remember, you are the creator of your life and you get to decide what hard work means to you. When you work hard and invest in yourself, luck will find you!

Now let's talk about how to take your passions and expertise and turn them into a six-figure business so you have even more time and money freedom...

CHAPTER 11

SIX FIGURES BUYS MORE FREEDOM

"Above all I learned that it's entirely possible for any one of us, with average intelligence, to increase our income without selling our soul."

~Barbara Stanny, author of
Secrets of Six-Figure Women

You don't have to work 60+ hours to make 6-figures. Many women mistakenly believe this.

I was only working about 20-25 hours per week in my outside sales job when I began making six figures and I had more time and money freedom than I ever had and I was loving life.

So, what changed? How did I go from making $50k to $100k+ working half the hours?

My mindset, my perspective, and my entire life was changed when I read Barbara Stanny's, *Secrets of Six-Figure Women: Surprising Strategies to Up Your Earnings and Change Your Life.* Barbara Stanny is also the author of many other books like *Overcoming Undearning* and one of my favorites,

Sacred Success. Her books have truly changed my life and I highly recommend them.

Barbara has such a fascinating story – her father was the "R" in H&R Block, a large and successful tax firm, and he was the founder of the company. She was raised to let men take care of the finances. Fast forward to when she got older, Barbara married a lousy Prince Charming and he lost a ton of Barbara's trust fund that had been set up for her by her father. After their divorce, she had huge tax bills, three small children, and a "brain incapable of deciphering financial jargon."

Today, Barbara Stanny is a high-income earner. She wrote the book, *Six Figure Women*, to learn the characteristics common in women making six figures. She interviewed 150 women, and that's how the book was created.

When you ask women if they want to make six figures, you usually get one of two replies:

1. **Sure, but *how* do I do that?**
2. **No, because I don't want to give up my soul to do it. I don't want to give up time with my family, friends, etc.**

The good news is you don't have to know the "how" and you don't have to sell your soul to make six figures. The reason I know this is because I've done it.

After leaving the legal field and finding Barbara Stanny's book, I was committed to becoming a six-figure woman. I started my website www.becomea6figurewoman.com when I began making six figures in 2005.

So how did I start making six figures and how long did it me?

¹ NOT focus on *how* it would happen. I simply commit- lf to making six figures and every day I would write

100 times in my journal *"I am making six figures doing what I love to do."*

We talked in an earlier chapter about the Reticular Activating System which brings relevant information to your attention and programs your subconscious. It's a powerful system that is built into our brains!

Here's how it works:

My goal and written affirmation was,, *"I am making six figures doing what I love to do."* Since I was NOT making six figures doing what I loved at the time, a *structural tension* was created in my brain. The brain always wants to resolve any structural tension. To do that, you will begin to draw to you what is needed to achieve the goal, which will in turn, resolve the structural tension.

Writing your goals down is key! Write them down in present tense as if you've already achieved them. Don't try to do this with ten goals. Just pick one for now. You can even use mine: *"I am making six figures doing what I love to do."*

It's not that you are going to sit back and do nothing, but now your RAS is at work and you will pay closer attention when you see six figure opportunities come your way.

Six Figures in 18 months

I created multiple streams of income doing a variety of jobs. I was reading the employment ads (this was back in the days before online job searching) in the Washington Post and one day I read an ad that said something like:

Make six figures working 20 hours a week selling a fun product. Play Golf. Enjoy Life. Call for more details.

Well, I didn't want to play golf, but I did want to make six figures working 20 hours a week.

I called about the job and found out it was an outside sales job selling hot tubs. I had no outside sales experience (17 years legal) and didn't know a thing about hot tubs. But what I did know was I wanted to make six figures doing what I loved.

I got on a call with one of the managers at the company and said, "Hi my name is Michelle Kulp, and I'm your next top salesperson!"

His reply was, "Do you have any in-home sales experience in a one-call close environment." The funny part was I didn't even know what a one-call close was!

I said something like, "Well not exactly, but I have other sales experience you will be interested in." He told me to fax over my resume' and he would be in touch. He was very short with me as I suspected he didn't believe I had the experience they were looking for.

So, I typed up a document called **"Top 10 Reasons Thermospas Should Hire Me,"** and I was very creative with that list.

I then created a new resume' that had every little thing I ever did in my entire life that involved sales; things like working at my dad's clothing store, Bond's Clothing, part-time as a teenager and selling products like Partylite and Christmas Around the World.

I was chosen as one of the 20 top picks by the company out of 200 applicants for an interview. I was the only female chosen (maybe because I was the only one who applied?) Apparently, this was a male-dominated field and it attracted a lot of experienced sales guys with lots of in-home, one-call close experience.

The interview was via teleconference at an office located in Washington, D.C. (the company was in Connecticut) and I felt pretty intimidated being around all these sales experts. When I walked into that meeting, I felt like I was out of my league; but I was committed to making six figures, so I stuck it out.

When it came my time for the interview, I was so nervous. I don't think I gave the politically correct answers they were looking for during the interview. The final question was: "Why do you think you would make a great in-home salesperson?"

My answer came from my heart: "Because I'm a kind and caring person. People warm up to me right away. I think if I had a quality product, backed by great company, that people would buy from me."

I went home after the interview and told my then boyfriend that I was certain I didn't get the job and that it was a colossal waste of time.

The next day I was surprised to get a call from the company telling me that I was chosen out of the 200 men that applied for the sales position. I was stunned. I said to the manager, "Can I ask you a question…how come out of all those experienced, highly qualified applicants, you decided to pick me?" His answer was "Because you don't have any bad habits."

They felt that people who worked in sales a long time had their own way of doing things and it would be easier to train a novice than to teach an old dog new tricks. Because I knew nothing about outside sales, they felt they could mold and train me how they wanted, and I would do well.

I'm happy to tell you, they were right! Within 18 months, I was making six figures. Was it easy? NO it was NOT. I had to memorize a 42-page script that I had to present in front of the President of the company, attend two weeks of hot tub boot camp in the factory learning all the technical and boring details about hot tubs, and I had to drive hundreds of miles to pre-confirmed appointments in an all-commission job. I can assure you it was not easy at first.

I decided to make it easier on myself and I started learning from the guys that were making six figures. There were a lot of guys struggling and complaining – I didn't hang out or talk to them. I didn't want them to bring me down. Instead, my focus was on the top income earners in the company. I learned everything I could from them.

Within six months of getting that job, there were weeks I wasn't making any money. I decided I was going to quit. So I called my manager and told him I was going to quit and find a *real job*. His reply was, "Michelle, there's about a year learning curve on this job. I promise you after a year, you will be one of our top sales reps."

He believed in me more than I believed in myself at the time. I was way out of my comfort zone, but I knew the potential was there to make six figures, so again, I stuck it out.

I did like driving to new towns, meeting new people and selling a fun product – hot tubs! We were the only company selling hot tubs in-home so we had no competition.

Within 18 months, I was making six figures and my life got so much easier. I had free time to work on my writing, teach classes, spend time with my kids, family and friends. I was also able to buy a house, pay off debt, and breathe.

I want to point out that it wasn't my "Dream" to be a hot tub sales rep, but it was a wonderful FREEDOM JOB that allowed me free time to work on my other dreams. It taught me valuable new sales skills that I could use in the marketplace and I had fun selling hot tubs! That job lasted 10 years until the housing market crashed and the company unfortunately filed bankruptcy.

After that, I had a decision to make. I was running my online business like a hobby with part-time income and I needed to replace my six-figure income. I took other sales jobs, but after eighteen months, I did not find a product or a company I was happy with. I made the decision that I was going to make six figures in my online business.

Of course, it didn't happen right away. As I mentioned, my income increased exponentially when I hired my first business coach, Jason Nyback, who changed my entire business and life. He was a brilliant business strategist, and within three months of working with him, my monthly online income skyrocketed!

In the previous chapter, we discussed investing in yourself – this was a massive investment in myself. I spent $6k to work with him for eight weeks, and then for the next four years I spent $1k per month ($12k per year) working with him. I probably didn't need to stay with him that long, but I loved working with him, and I was always learning so much.

I don't have the exact details about how you can make six figures, but I know that if you commit to making six figures doing what you love and investing in yourself, that it will happen for you.

THE LOWDOWN ON LOW EARNERS

An underearner is anyone who earns below their potential. I am a recovering underearner for sure.

Here's some of the traits of underearners according to Barbara Stanny:

- ✓ **Underearners have a high tolerance for low pay** – high earners normally lean towards more lucrative fields. If you don't go where there's a potential to make money, it doesn't matter how hard you work.

- ✓ **Underearners underestimate their worth** – They feel that life is unfair and they are disadvantaged as compared to the "privileged group."

✓ **Underearners are willing to work for free** – Underearners give away their time, knowledge and skills for nothing.

✓ **Underearners are lousy negotiators** – Underearners are reluctant to ask for more and let fear control them.

✓ **Underearners practice reverse snobbery** – They believe that people who have a lot of money are greedy, insensitive and feel superior.

✓ **Underearners believe in the nobility of poverty** – Many of them take great pride in barely making a living and believe it's more noble to be one of the poor.

✓ **Underearners are subtle self-saboteurs** – They throw banana peels in their own path in a variety of ways: applying for work they're not qualified for, creating problems with coworkers, procrastinating or leaving projects unfinished, stopping short of reaching their goals. The common thread is their propensity to be scattered, distracted, and/or unfocused.

✓ **Underearners are unequivocally codependent** – They put other people's dreams ahead of their own and are the sacrificial lamb. They have weak boundaries and put themselves last at the sake of others.

✓ **Underearners are in financial chaos** – They go from crisis to crisis, constantly moving money from one account to another, borrowing from Peter to pay Paul and heading toward financial disaster.

Do any of these sound familiar? If so, you too are probably an underearner.

CHARACTERISTICS OF AN UNDEREARNER:

- Negative feelings about money.
- Work very long hours or have several jobs to make ends meet.
- Fill your free time with endless chores, tasks, or television.
- Are in debt with little or No savings.
- Have no idea where your money is going.
- Have a family history of debt and/or underearning.
- Put others needs ahead of your own.
- Are in financial pain or stress.
- Give away your knowledge and services for free.
- Undercharge for your services.
- Avoid dealing with money.
- Find it hard to ask for a raise.
- Blame others for your financial situation.
- Are proud of your ability to make do with little.

When I read Barbara Stanny's book, it opened my eyes to the fact that I was a classic underearner. It's taken years of working on these issues, becoming educated and most importantly, implementing what I've learned. Of course, there's still more to improve. It's not a one-and-done event. It's a life-long process.

Self-improvement is ongoing. I believe the purpose of life is to evolve and that the top of one mountain is the bottom of another. I'm always ascending up the ladder.

Don't read this chapter and feel bad about where you are. Knowledge and self-awareness are power.

If you want to quit your job, it's important to take action and make the necessary changes in your financial house so you can live your dreams.

You can make six figures doing what you love. I am living proof of that. You don't have to work 60-80 hours a week as some people inaccurately believe or sell your soul. You can get paid to do what you love. First, figure out what you love and make sure there is a demand for that in the marketplace, and then charge what you're worth.

The more you do what you love, the better you get at it and, the more money you will make. I didn't start out making six figures online, but once I mastered a lot of skills, the value I gave to others kept increasing and so did the money I was earning.

RECOMMENDED RESOURCES:

- Dave Ramsey's Financial Peace University: www.daveramsey.com/fpu

- Any of Barbara Stanny's books or classes (she married recently and has changed her name to Barbara Huson) https://www.barbara-huson.com/

Now, it's time for our final chapter on this journey. Taking the leap and planning your exit strategy!

CHAPTER 12

YOUR 6-STEP EXIT STRATEGY

"Letting go is death.
People think leaving a job is about leaving a
job. It's about leaving a life, a history, a context,
a cubbyhole, the only person you knew how to
be, and the one everybody loved."

~Tama J. Kieves, author of
This Time I Dance! Trusting the Journey of
Creating the Work you Love

Imagine no more rush hour traffic, no more long commutes, no more deadlines, no more overtime, no more missing family events, dinners, and no more bosses! And more time with your family, money in the bank, and most importantly, more time to enjoy life.

The challenge is to make more money and work less hours so that you can devote your life to pursuing the dreams you have for you and your family.

In order to declare financial independence from wage slavery, you need an EXIT STRATEGY.

6-STEP EXIT STRATEGY FOR QUITTING YOUR JOB

This is a summary of what you've been learning throughout this book. When you put everything together, this is your exit strategy.

STEP 1: PREPARE YOUR FINANCES

Your finances MUST be in order before you quit your job to do work that is meaningful and more fulfilling, even if it's transitioning from full-time to part- time work; or going from a BONDAGE JOB to a FREEDOM JOB; or quitting your job completely in order to do what you love. If you don't get your finances in order, you will have high stress. Ideally, your debt is zero, except for your living expenses, and you have at least one year of expenses in the bank (preferably 18 months if you can swing it). Don't sit back and do nothing and draw on your savings. Have your savings there for peace of mind knowing that if needed, you can survive 12-18 months if everything falls apart.

STEP 2: HAVE A WRITTEN DOWN INCOME PLAN

In the previous chapters, I recommended testing out your dream job, making your first $100 from some of your ideas, and even hiring a consultant at Pivot Planet to get all the details of what that job or business is like. By nature, some businesses are feast or famine. I know because my online business was like that for a long time. When I finally hired my business coach in 2014, I was generating leads by running paid Facebook ads to an automated webinar, but it was expensive.

However, many times when you're starting out, you don't have a huge marketing budget. I don't do any paid advertising now because all of my business comes from referrals.

That's because I've spent years developing relationships and I've been doing this work long enough that referrals come in consistently. So, if you're starting your own business, you need to know where you will find your new clients. If you're transitioning from one job to another job, then you know where your income is coming from. I recommend at least two streams of income to start. Remember that done-for-you services are much easier to get your income flowing right away if you're going down the entrepreneurial path. Write down your monthly income goals, your expenses, and your plan for getting leads and clients. Read this plan every day. Even if your transitioning to a new job, I want you to have a minimum of two streams of income.

STEP 3: PREPARE YOUR BREAK-UP SPEECH

Your boss is most likely going to ask why you're quitting. There's no need to get into specifics or to say things like "Because I hate you, this company, and everyone in it!" Instead, just voice your appreciation for the opportunities the company gave you with something like this: "I am very grateful for having my job for the last ** years, and I've learned so much working here. However, at this point in my career, I'm excited to contribute my skills to another company where I can make an impact on a different level." Or "I am very grateful for having my job for the last ** years and I've learned so much working here. However, at this point in my career, I'm excited to branch out on my own to do something different." Even if you are starting a company similar to the one you're leaving, don't let them know that. Of course, if you have a non-compete agreement with that company, you must consult a lawyer if the business you are starting is the same or similar. But if you're leaving your job to do your own thing in a different field, there is no need to give them details. Unless of course, you think that your boss could give you referrals, then by all means have that conversation.

STEP 4: PREPARE YOURSELF FOR A COUNTEROFFER

It's sad to say, but many times when you try to quit your job, the company will offer you more money, a promotion, better benefits, etc. Of course, that leaves you feeling angry wondering why they didn't give you that before if they valued you so highly. The truth is, it's not their fault; it's yours for not asking. It doesn't mean they would have given it to you, but many times as underearners we settle for much less than we're worth. Then we make this huge decision and commitment to quit our jobs and the company offers us more money. Very frustrating! Stick to your plan and thank your boss for the offer but tell him or her your mind is made up. It's good to know this is a possibility before you have the break-up conversation so you don't react impulsively.

STEP 5: SCHEDULE THE BREAK-UP

The day is finally here, and you are going to give the required notice because you don't want to burn any bridges. Also do this in person, not via text or email or social media. Even though you may have fantasies of quitting your job without any notice and making a scene, it's not a good idea. You want good karma as you quit your job. Make sure you ask for a reference if the conversation goes well as it could be useful down the road as you move on to your new life.

STEP 6: PREPARE FOR A MOURNING PERIOD

This last step in your exit strategy is preparing yourself for a period of grieving and mourning. Even if you didn't LOVE your job, there will be period of mourning and the death of your old life. This mourning period can last a few weeks to a few months or even more. My identity for 17+ years was wrapped around the law, being a paralegal, working in the legal environment and the structure my job provided. I wasn't just leaving a job; I was leaving life as I knew it. It's important to mourn the loss of your title, your co-workers, your schedule, your paycheck, your benefits, and who you showed up as in the world. It's also really scary because you now have a blank slate on which to create a new life.

WOBBLING AND UNCERTAINTY ARE GOOD SIGNS

I wrote this book as a "12-month Guide to Being Joyfully Jobless" because I want you to know you can't just snap your figures and be magically transported into a new life. You have to do the work and *the work* takes time. No one can do it for you.

Just know that you will wobble with uncertainty as you take this journey to freedom, but it's better to wobble than to settle for a life of mediocrity.

It helps to have a mindset like a little child who is exploring the world with new eyes for the first time and trying to understand it and figure things out. You will never have all the answers or a fail-proof plan.

You are being called to walk off the beaten path, and I'm here to gently remind you some days you will question your sanity. Just remember that you have an inner guidance system

(IGS) that you can access any time when you are feeling over-whelmed or overcome with fear. Your very own IGS will give you all the answers you need when you slow down, get still and listen to it.

When my job at the law firm ended, I had no idea what I was going to do to pay the bills and take care of my three children, but the more I learned to listen to my own inner guidance system, the more I began to find my way, follow my heart and live my dreams.

Uncertainty is the first step to our freedom. Knowing that we don't *know* the way, accepting that fully and having faith that the teachers we need will appear on the path as we begin travelling to unexplored worlds.

You'll never have a magical life that has 100% certainty in it. That's the point. When you have FAITH, then the MAGIC appears.

TRUST.

*****

THE END OF THIS BOOK = THE BEGINNING OF YOUR NEW LIFE

If you've gotten this far then I know you are serious in your quest to discover and live those dreams of yours. You can connect with me at: **www.becomea6figurewoman.com**

Never, ever give up on Your Dreams!

Michelle Kulp

CAN YOU DO ME A FAVOR

Before you go, I'd like to say thank you for purchasing my book. I really appreciate it!

I'd like to ask a small favor. *Would you take a minute or two to leave a review for this book on Amazon?*

This feedback will help me continue to write the kind of books that help inspire, motivate and educate people to believe in themselves and to find their true purpose in life.

If you enjoyed my book, then please let me know ☺

Michelle Kulp

Made in the USA
Coppell, TX
18 March 2020